Deep transformations

Manchester University Press

PROGRESS IN POLITICAL ECONOMY

Series editors: Andreas Bieler (School of Politics and International Relations, University of Nottingham), Gareth Bryant (Department of Political Economy at the University of Sydney), Mònica Clua-Losada (Department of Political Science, University of Texas Rio Grande Valley), Adam David Morton (Department of Political Economy, University of Sydney), and Angela Wigger (Department of Political Science, Radboud University, The Netherlands).

Since its launch in 2014, the blog Progress in Political Economy (PPE) – available at www.ppesydney.net/ – has become a central forum for the dissemination and debate of political economy research published in book and journal article forms with crossover appeal to academic, activist and public policy related audiences.

Now the Progress in Political Economy book series with Manchester University Press provides a new space for innovative and radical thinking in political economy, covering interdisciplinary scholarship from the perspectives of critical political economy, historical materialism, feminism, political ecology, critical geography, heterodox economics, decolonialism and racial capitalism.

The PPE book series combines the reputations and reach of the PPE blog and MUP as a publisher to launch critical political economy research and debates. We welcome manuscripts that realise the very best new research from established scholars and early-career scholars alike.

Previously published titles

Deep transformations

A theory of degrowth

Hubert Buch-Hansen, Max Koch
and Iana Nesterova

MANCHESTER UNIVERSITY PRESS

Published by Manchester University Press
Oxford Road, Manchester, M13 9PL

www.manchesteruniversitypress.co.uk

British Library Cataloguing-in-Publication Data
A catalogue record for this book is available from the British
Library

ISBN 978 1 5261 7326 3 hardback
ISBN 978 1 5261 7785 8 paperback

First published 2024

Typeset by Newgen Publishing UK

To Krista

Contents

Tables

Introduction: leaving the path towards eco-social collapse

Contemporary societies face several deep and intertwined crises. The level of economic inequality has reached staggering heights. While a small elite has accumulated wealth on an unprecedented scale, many people lack the means to satisfy even their basic human needs. Economic and financial downturns only further these inequalities and divides. At the same time, democratic institutions are increasingly being undermined. Social scientists now contemplate how democracy will end (Runciman 2018), they speak of the rise of authoritarian forms of neoliberalism (Bruff 2014; Wigger 2019), and suggest that even in countries where democracy used to be strongly established, we find ourselves on the path towards post-democracy (Crouch 2016).

On top of social, health and political crises come the catastrophic ecological and biodiversity crises (Ceballos et al. 2015). A number of planetary boundaries, including climate change, loss of biosphere integrity, landsystem change and biogeochemical cycles, are being transgressed (Steffen et al. 2015). Overall, then, contemporary societies exist within a complex constellation of deeply interrelated and mutually intensifying crises spanning multiple dimensions of being. An outcome of these crises is that the preconditions for human beings and other species to thrive – and indeed live – are rapidly being undermined.

The root cause of the crises, whether directly or indirectly, is the capitalist organisation of societies and the capitalist growth imperative central to this organisation (Foster et al. 2010). Capitalism is a system of human organisation which orientates all human activities and pursuits towards valorisation of capital (Gorz 2012). The engine of capitalism is the process of capital accumulation, that is, the microeconomic activity of reinvestment of past profits motivated by the desire to make more profits. This process translates into economic growth, upon which capitalism is structurally reliant for its functioning. The accumulate-or-die logic defining capitalism as an economic system creates a constant pressure to expand market relations into new domains and to intensify such relations where they already exist.

The result is both the geographical spread of the capital relation, which has reached its culmination in globalised capitalism, and the ever-deeper exploitation of human beings and nature. Even spiritual traditions and practices such as mindfulness and meditation are not immune to commercialisation and utilisation for the purpose of increased labour productivity (Purser 2019).

Seen in a historical perspective, the climate and biodiversity crises are inevitable outcomes of the functioning of capitalism. The global economy's long-term exponential growth has resulted in an economy that is far too large relative to the biosphere and thus grossly unsustainable (Koch 2012). While capitalism is pervaded by several contradictions (Harvey 2014), today the main contradiction in the capital relation is that between capital and nature (Jessop and Morgan 2022). Latouche (2009: 2) observes that we find ourselves in 'a performance car that has no driver, no reverse gear and no brakes and it is going to slam into the limitations of the planet'. One would perhaps think that this situation would prompt large electoral majorities, policymakers, economists, investors, business associations and labour unions to seriously take stock of the situation and consider whether the time has come to replace the 'car' (capitalism) with an altogether different model. Yet, while awareness of the looming ecological collapse has increased in recent times, the pro-growth discourse remains hegemonic. According to the currently prevailing perception, the only viable way forward is to pursue so-called green growth, that is, continued economic growth combined with protection of 'environmental services'. Underlying this notion is a fundamental optimism as to what technologies and capitalist markets can accomplish. New innovations coupled with various forms of market-based solutions are expected to lead to greener production, greener jobs, greener consumption and greener growth, all of which will reduce inequalities and environmental impacts – not least CO_2 emissions.[1]

Appealing as this vision may seem, the available evidence does not suggest that it is in fact possible, in the available time and on a global scale, to combine economic growth with rapidly declining CO_2 emissions (Haberl et al. 2020; Jackson 2016). The developments thus far certainly give no reason for optimism: for all the green innovations that have appeared and despite political pledges to halt emissions, CO_2 levels in the atmosphere have continued to break new records (Buller 2022). Little suggests that this is about to change in any fundamental way, let alone in good time: in 2018, an IPCC report suggested that we had 12 years to initiate far-reaching change (IPCC 2018). With no profound shift having occurred, this 'window of opportunity' has narrowed to seven years. The main achievement of the green growth idea has been to greenwash, and thus contribute to the reproduction of, the capitalist economy and mode of living. All the while capitalism is being 'green-growth washed' by the powers that be at the level of discourse; business as, by and large, usual continues at the level of material reality.

The great paradox of our times is this: on one hand it is increasingly unlikely that capitalism can survive the multiple crises confronting it (Streeck 2016). One aspect of this is that, in its destruction and degradation of nature, it is ultimately endangering its own continued existence because it is but a subsystem of nature.[2] On the other hand, while the level of awareness of the climate and biodiversity crises is now relatively high (Brand and Wissen 2013), capitalist ideology is so prevalent that most people continue to find it impossible to conceive of a world without capitalism and exponential economic growth, let alone imagine that another economic system could work better. And those who can imagine a different system, one in which capital is not akin to a deity and humans are not reduced to mere consumers, may struggle to envision how such a system could come into being.

In this situation, critical scholarship has crucial roles to play. These roles include, for instance, showing how there's nothing natural or inevitable about current socio-economic arrangements, developing visions of different socio-economic orders and theorising how they may materialise.

The present book concerns one important vision of a different type of society, a vision that involves leaving the path towards eco-social collapse that humanity is currently heading down. This vision, which goes by the name of *degrowth*, has gained considerable momentum among scholars, activists and practitioners in recent times. Degrowth entails societies in which much is different – including, for example, work, production, consumption, housing, prevailing values, gender roles, the distribution of resources and decision-making processes (Buch-Hansen and Nesterova 2023). A mushrooming literature revolves around the degrowth vision and countless policies and other initiatives that can move current societies in the direction of degrowth are being discussed in recent years. This literature often paints a picture of a better future, where human needs are satisfied, where community replaces commerce (Klitgaard 2013), where humans participate in creative, meaningful and fulfilling activities (Trainer 2012) and where nature and non-humans thrive. While such a future appears highly attractive compared to what we are currently heading towards, the question remains: how do we get there? Various ideas exist, but degrowth transformations have yet to be theorised in a manner taking into account the complexity and depth of reality.

The present book contributes to filling this gap. It develops a theory of deep transformations for degrowth via a combination of insights from political economy, feminism, human geography, anarchism and sociology, among other perspectives, and grounds this emerging theory in the ontology of critical realist philosophy. From a critical realist perspective, the purpose of theory is to bring to the surface constellations of mechanisms which cause, or have a potential to cause, specific outcomes and phenomena. An interdisciplinary and holistic theorisation is required due to the enormous diversity and complexity that characterises modern societies and that would therefore also characterise degrowth transformations. The theory thus considers the multiple and overlapping planes, scales and sites on which degrowth transformations would need to unfold. The *planes* include humanity's transactions with nature, social interactions, social structures and peoples' inner being (Bhaskar 2016). The *scales* include the local, the national and the transnational levels on which political struggles alongside other processes would take place. The *sites* include civil society, business and the state.

Before expanding on the content of the book, the next two sections unfold the notion of degrowth and introduce the critical realist ontology underpinning the theory.

What is degrowth?

The ideas explored by degrowth scholars have long intellectual heritages and stories. For instance, calls for simpler and more harmonious living, deviation from consumerism and seeing non-humans as neighbours can readily be found in the nineteenth century (see e.g., Thoreau 2016). Likewise, the need to live harmoniously in and with nature was highlighted (Emerson 2009a, 2009b) and the 'hunger for wealth, which reduces the planet to a garden' was noticed in the same century (Emerson 2009b: 161). Going even further back in history, in ancient China the obligation of the government to ensure that human needs are met and for the people to develop human qualities such as benevolence and moral agency were outlined (Mote 1989).

The end of economic growth was an issue considered by several of the classical political economists. Among these, John Stuart Mill stood out by believing that the emergence of a non-growing economy could be 'a very considerable improvement on our present condition' and that 'there would be as much scope as ever for all kinds of mental culture, and moral and social progress; as much room for improving the Art of Living, and much more likelihood of its being improved, when minds ceased to be engrossed by the art of getting on' (Mill 1848: book IV, chapter VI).

The notion of degrowth (*décroissance*) is more recent. It was coined by French political ecologist André Gorz in the early 1970s. In a later work he observes that 'today a lack of realism no longer consists in advocating greater well-being through the inversion of growth and the subversion of the prevailing way of life. Lack of realism consists in imagining that economic growth can still bring about increased human welfare, and indeed that it is still physically possible' (Gorz 1980: 14). From the outset, then, degrowth formed part of a critique, an opposition, a discourse of deviation from the pursuit of economic growth and hence from the destruction of life on earth. It opposed capitalism with its growth imperative, its ever-increasing production and consumption, its overuse of material and energy resources, its exploitation of human and non-human life and beings, its commercialisation of almost everything. Having laid dormant for many years, the concept of degrowth was revived in the new millennium. This happened in France where Serge Latouche emerged as a leading proponent of degrowth and where the first international degrowth conference took place in 2008. Over the past decade or so, degrowth has become a concept around which both the works of a fast-growing number of researchers and the activities of an international social movement have come to revolve.

The concept of degrowth does not have a single definition or meaning that all advocates of it equally accept. However, there is broad consensus that the energy and matter throughput of the rich countries is to decrease significantly, and that this shrinking process would need to be organised democratically and without undermining critical levels of wellbeing. One matter that deserves to be highlighted is that degrowth, despite its (perhaps unfortunate) name, is not opposed to growth per se (Buch-Hansen and Nesterova 2023). Degrowth is consistent with certain forms of *non-material growth*. These include growth in everything that can be associated with the goodness of human nature, such as care, solidarity, mutual aid, empathy, creativity and imagination, cooperation, connectedness, consciousness and attention, concern for others, and benevolence. Some forms of *material growth* also resonate with degrowth, the reason being that degrowth targets *aggregate growth*. For instance, selective growth in desirable industries (such as in renewable energy provision, organic agriculture and permaculture) is necessary. So are improvements in material conditions, material consumption and access to infrastructure for those whose genuine needs are not met. Such needs include basic needs as well as needs for education, self-realisation and even spirituality. Yet another type of growth that does not go against degrowth is growth in alternatives and in the diversity of forms of production. This is something diverse economies scholars have researched and described extensively throughout recent decades (e.g., Gibson-Graham 2006; Gibson-Graham and Dombroski 2020). The diverse economies approach identifies a wide variety of non-capitalist options which currently exist in, and even sustain, capitalist societies, and which can become essential parts of the landscape of degrowth societies. In terms of the forms of production, for instance, they may include cooperatives, artisanal production and foraging.

Further to these reflections, degrowth can be seen to imply a reduction in humanity's use of the material and energy resources wherever it can be done, growth in their use where necessary, growth in diversity and growth in human qualities in pursuit of harmonious coexistence. Naturally, when such equal access to resources (material and immaterial) and satisfaction of needs are pursued and when growth in the non-material is encouraged, it precludes capitalistic strivings. By definition, then, degrowth cannot be capitalist. Apart from being anti-capitalist in seeking to transform all capitalist forms of social being and human organisation, degrowth is also a process which does not define itself purely in terms of being against, but also in terms of continuously and adventurously being for. Throughout the book we emphasise this processual and fundamentally hopeful and positive character of degrowth. Finally, we perceive degrowth as a phenomenon that, far from merely involving less and different consumption and production, involves deep change on all planes of social being. We return to this matter in the next section when we outline the ontology underpinning the theory of degrowth transformations.

As noted above, a growing field of research revolves around the concept of degrowth. Initially, the main scientific base of this field was political ecology and especially ecological economics. In contrast to mainstream neoclassical economics, ecological economics regards the economy to be a subsystem of society, which in turn is a subsystem of nature (Spangenberg 2016). As a result, there are natural limits as to how big the economy can grow. To ecological economists, economic growth denotes 'an increase in the physical scale of matter/energy throughput that sustains the economic activities of production and consumption of commodities' (Daly 1996: 31). Considering that throughput has grown far too big relative to the capacity of the biosphere, they argue that it is necessary to drastically reduce throughput in the rich countries. While it is the expectation that doing so will mean a reduction of GDP (the standard measure of economic activity), the *goal* is not a GDP reduction (Kallis 2018).

These insights of ecological economics are widely embraced by degrowth scholars. Yet with the growth of the degrowth research field, its scientific base has broadened considerably. Sociologists (e.g., Koch 2022a), political economists (e.g., Buch-Hansen 2014; Chertkovskaya et al. 2019), geographers (see e.g., Schmid 2018) and scholars from many other disciplines now work with the concept of degrowth, resulting in a highly diverse and interdisciplinary body of scholarship. Degrowth has been put in conversations with a wide range of perspectives, including, for instance, feminism (Dengler and Seebacher 2019), historical materialism (Leonardi 2019), diverse economies thinking (Schmid 2020), existentialism (Nesterova 2021a) and critical realism (Bhaskar et al. 2012; Buch-Hansen and Nesterova 2021, 2023;

see also Morgan 2021 and Schoppek 2020). Moreover, degrowth thinking has been applied to and related with multiple phenomena, such as business and organisation (Hankammer et al. 2021; Nesterova 2020a, 2021a; Schmid 2018, 2020), housing (Mete and Xue 2021), social policy (Koch 2022b), urban planning (Xue 2021) and technology (Heikkurinen 2018).[3]

A *social movement* calling for degrowth emerged in the context of the first international degrowth conferences. The conferences, which continue to take place regularly, bring together activists, artists and academics – and conference contributions span both conventional presentations of research and various forms of activism. More generally, a wide variety of movements can be seen as degrowth compatible (Burkhart et al. 2020). Implicitly degrowth-compatible movements such as voluntary simplicity, the tiny house movement and the zero-waste movement have many commonalities with degrowth, but do not identify themselves as degrowth, though some of the people within those movements might do or generally share degrowth sentiments, arguments and pursuits.

Degrowth can also be regarded as a diverse *political project*. It is diverse because despite sharing the critique of capitalism and having a desire to achieve harmonious coexistence, views as regards the means by which such coexistence can be achieved differ. Some perceive degrowth to be an eco-socialist project (Swift 2014). Others advocate anarchism (Trainer 2014) and call for change in individuals' values and worldviews first and foremost (Nesterova 2021a, 2021b). Still others do not propose a single political ideology but rather highlight the variety of political systems, and hence propose a variety of pathways through which degrowth can be achieved in practice, which include both top-down and bottom-up strategies or a combination of eco-socialist and anarchist means.

The journey(s) of degrowth as a field of research, a social movement and a political project is ongoing. It is motivated by a shared desire for a better future, for a lasting, harmonious, peaceful co-existence between humanity and nature, between humans and non-humans, and within humanity, which includes one's own self (Bonnedahl and Heikkurinen 2019; Nesterova 2021a). In the field of research, the collection of knowledge is deepening and becoming broader. Yet degrowth scholarship also remains a collection of often dispersed and contradictory knowledge and it still lacks a solid foundation in the social sciences. Deepening of degrowth knowledge is done from a variety of philosophical standpoints (whether explicit or implicit), which, while not being bad in itself, often makes degrowth knowledge(s) incompatible. The breadth of degrowth knowledge makes it increasingly challenging to know what degrowth is and what it is not. Without a solid foundation in the social sciences, degrowth risks going down the path of remaining a mostly academic social movement rather than becoming at once an established and influential academic paradigm, a successful and attractive political project and, of course, an inclusive and effective social movement. For the social scientific foundations to be solid, philosophical underpinnings need to be explicated.

The planes of social being

Any social scientific theory incorporates a set of ontological assumptions, that is, assumptions about the general nature of social being. The social ontology accompanying a theory regulates the type of explanations we can provide when applying it. For example, a structuralist ontology precludes agency-oriented explanations. It is thus crucially important that a theory aspiring to provide a holistic perspective on degrowth transformations is underpinned by a comprehensive and anti-reductionist ontology, that is, an ontology that recognises social being in its entirety, including its relation to nature, and which reduces no aspect of social reality (say, the activities of agents) to a by-product of another (say, culture). We contend that the critical realist perspective in the philosophy of science, and specifically Roy Bhaskar's *four planes of social being model* (Bhaskar 1986, 1993, 2016), offers precisely such an ontology. Indeed, Bhaskar's philosophy of science perspective is distinct in that it starts out from deep ontological reflections based on which it subsequently develops its perspective on the form and purpose of (social) scientific knowledge. The reason why this specific sequence is advocated is that it makes little sense to take a position on what forms knowledge should take without having first reflected on the overall nature of the reality that this knowledge concerns (Bhaskar 2008). In what follows, we briefly outline the ontology underpinning our theory of degrowth transformations (for a general introduction to critical realism, see Buch-Hansen and Nielsen 2020).

Critical realist ontology covers both physical and social realities, considering them to be deep and layered. In the present context, we focus on *social* ontology as we consider it particularly relevant in relation to degrowth. After all, transformations need to happen in social reality, whereas nature needs to become subject to transformation as little as possible. The conceptualisation of the relationship between structure and agency is of crucial importance to the analysis of social change and stability. It has thus attracted attention ever since the beginning of the social sciences and is also at the heart of critical realist social ontology (Bhaskar 1998; Archer 1995). Reductionist approaches that privilege structure over agency or vice versa have traditionally prevailed. Yet several social theorists, including, for example, Marx, Giddens and Bourdieu, occupy various types of middle positions in the social structures/individual actions continuum (Koch 2020a).

Critical realism also advocates a specific type of middle position, according to which the social structures confronting human beings are never made in the present by those same human beings, but are the outcome of human activities undertaken in the past. In the words of Bhaskar (1998: 45–46), 'people do not create society. For it always pre-exists them and is a necessary condition for their activity. Rather, society must be regarded as an ensemble of structures, practices and conventions which individuals reproduce or transform, but which would not exist unless they did so'. The social structures of today face us as an objective reality and they are not going to disappear so that new structures can be created. The implication for a theoretically informed analysis of degrowth transformations is that it needs to start out from currently existing structures. Not only do these structures condition agency, future degrowth societies would also evolve from them.

Burkhart et al. (2020: 18) note that degrowth movements generally 'share a holistic image of human beings, which they express either explicitly or implicitly. People are not seen as rational utility maximisers à la homo oeconomicus, but rather as social and emotional beings living in relationships with and depending on each other.' This view of human beings is consistent with the ontology of critical realism. The latter emphasises that while agency is conditioned by structure, it is never determined by it. Although they are ontologically dependent, social structures and people are fundamentally different from each other (Bhaskar 1998: 42). Like structures, people are different. But unlike structures, people have identities, emotions, intentions and reasons. Unlike structures, people can be reflexive, creative, loving, aggressive and impatient. And unlike structures, people have the capacity to exercise agency, understood as intentional causality (Bhaskar 1998). These are important insights in relation to degrowth transformations as they suggest that human beings – through concerted actions – are able to change currently existing social structures. A key task of the theoretical perspective to be outlined in this book is to fill this and other ontological statements with sociological content to render more concrete the nature of, and pathways to, change. For example, drawing on Pierre Bourdieu, we propose that some groups are more likely to be in favour of degrowth than are others.

Whereas Bhaskar's initial thinking on social ontology to a large extent centred on the agency–structure relationship, subsequently he expanded it and proposed that social being – that is, any social phenomenon, event or person – exists (is and is in becoming) simultaneously on four social planes (Bhaskar 1986: 128–130, 2016: 53). The planes are interconnected and include (a) material transactions with nature, (b) social interactions between people/inter-subjectivities, (c) social structure and (d) the inner being of individuals. Viewing social being as existing and unfolding on the four planes at

once is valuable for degrowth because it provides a holistic and, by definition, anti-reductionist perspective. It precludes simple answers and unsustainable or unrealistic solutions. Degrowth transformations will concern all
planes of social being. Transactions with nature (a) need to be improved via
a (selective and equitable) reduction in matter and energy throughout. Social
interactions between people (b) need to become more humane (involving
for instance caring, empathy, solidarity, kindness, generosity and tolerance
of diversity) as opposed to taking capitalist forms (exploitation, competition). Social structures (c) need to undergo a significant transformation, for
instance involving redistribution of resources to massively reduce economic
inequality. Human selves (d) are where unprecedented *growth* needs to happen. After all, transformation arises from human agents: 'agency provides
the effective causes for what happens in society – only human beings can act'
(Danermark et al. 2002: 12).

Human agents are cultural beings (Tuan 2001). Culture is often defined
in opposition to nature (Benton 2001). In the words of Benton (2001: 137),
such 'opposition renders literally unthinkable the complex processes of
interaction, interpenetration and mutual constitution which link together
the items which are misleadingly dissociated from one another and allocated
abstractly to one side or other of the Nature/Culture great divide'. In the
course of degrowth transformation(s), one task is to overcome this opposition which permeates all four planes of social beings. Currently, nature is
seen as a collection of resources (plane a), social interactions and structures
(planes b and c) are seen as separate from nature or human-made, while
the embodiment of personality is viewed through the lens of mind–body
(Cartesian) dualism. Degrowth should aim to transcend such dualism by
recognising our ultimate dependence on nature and a deep interconnection
with it. Even as individual humans we are not only em-bodied, but also em-
placed, and the nature of the place co-creates our subjectivity (Næss 2016).
Such em-placement refers not only to a person's immediate location, but
also to the cosmos at large (Tuan 2013), that is, nature includes existence
far beyond the nature in one's region or even the earth.

As Bhaskar pointed out, one immediate virtue of the four-planar model 'is
that it pinpoints the ecological dimension of social being that social theorists
have been prone to ignore' (2016: 83). Displacing human beings from the
central position in ontology and incorporating the human being as well as
humanity as a whole into nature indicates transcending anthropocentrism.
Critical realism taken seriously and to its latest stage (the philosophy of
metaReality; see Bhaskar 2012a, 2012b) calls for and can effectively under-
pin a holistic and processual theory of transformation. The four-planar
model is, as is ontology in general, formulated at a high (philosophical)
level of abstraction. It is the task of substantive theory to render concrete

the nature of the structures, agents, interactions, cultures etc. on the various planes that matter in relation to whatever phenomenon the theory concerns.

As noted above, the theory to be developed in this book proposes that degrowth transformations will unfold on various planes, scales and sites. As the four planes encompass social being in its totality, both the scales and sites exist within each of them. For instance, material transactions with nature concern the local, the regional, the national and the international scales. Improving material transactions with nature on the local scale while causing damage elsewhere is not a degrowth transformation. Likewise, policies which improve the state of affairs for the local population while destroying livelihoods elsewhere should not be considered degrowth compatible. The concept of a site brings our attention to places which may be small and otherwise overlooked when theorising planes, scales and places with their own lasting constellation of structures and relationships. For instance, a human individual can be a site of transformation where a different mode of being can be nurtured and a different way of relating with the world can be encouraged. We identify and theorise three interconnected but relatively well-defined sites of transformation: civil society (including human individuals), state and business. Naturally, such sites can take different forms, and degrowth journeys will depend on this form.

Further to its deep ontology, critical realism advocates the view that social scientific practice should illuminate causal mechanisms, including underlying social structures, cultures and agency. An analysis of degrowth transformations underpinned by critical realism should thus aspire to illuminate both the mechanisms that make current societies in the rich countries grossly unsustainable, and the mechanisms needed to bring about degrowth transitions in specific settings. No individual discipline can on its own capture the nature of multidimensional degrowth transformations. Psychology, sociology, political economy, ecology, geography and other disciplines thus all need to participate in the uncovering of possibilities for (time- and place-sensitive) transformations.

A final feature of the critical realist philosophy of science perspective to be mentioned here is that it views normativity as a necessary and significant part of scientific practice (Bhaskar et al. 2010). In Bhaskar's view, social science can come to be emancipatory by illuminating constraining social structures that sustain various ills in social life, structures that people may be unaware of (Bhaskar 1998: 32). For example, while some aspects of social being across the four planes are clear to people, others may be less obvious. A human being may have a sense of selfhood or individuality, but may find it less clear which social structures influence his/her life and how. It becomes a responsibility of social scientists to explicate such structures and look deeply into social phenomena while critiquing oppressive structures and false knowledge, including capitalist myths. Cases in point are the myths that one is poor because of laziness and that consumption makes one happy. Degrowth is also orientated towards emancipation, including liberation from the constraints imposed onto human beings and non-humans by capitalism. Thus, degrowth research in general – and the theory of transformation outlined in the chapters that follow – has much to gain from being rooted in a philosophy of science perspective that can bolster such critical aspirations, legitimising them as constituting a key feature of scientific practice.

On the content of this book

The purpose of this book is to propose a scientifically and philosophically informed, holistic account of degrowth-inspired change: a theory of deep transformations. By introducing the reader to the four planes of social being, we hope to encourage the academic community, policymakers, activists and practitioners to become attentive to the depths and connectedness of social reality both within itself and with nature, and when facing complexity to go beyond labelling something as 'complex', attempting instead to disentangle and theoretically structure complexity. When contemplating transformations, this involves, for instance, avoiding placing hope, resources and efforts into any single policy, pursuit or place, and when indeed targeting any particular aspects of social reality, to ask oneself, what does it mean for other planes, scales and sites?

The book starts out from an account of capitalism both in its general and specific forms (Chapters 1 and 2). In Chapter 1, drawing mainly on Marx but also on other social theorists, we consider the growth imperative and the nature of work and consumption in capitalism. Moreover, we reflect upon capitalism in relation to (human) nature. Chapter 2 introduces the notion of institutional forms to consider capitalism as it actually manifests itself in concrete places and time periods. The notion is subsequently used to reflect upon possible features of degrowth societies and economies. In Chapter 3 we initiate the theorisation of deep transformations. Drawing inspiration mainly from contemporary political economy scholarship, we distil various prerequisites for transformative change, including a deep crisis, the articulation of a political project, the mobilisation of a comprehensive coalition of social forces and the building of consent.

The following three chapters enrich the theorisation by zooming in on the sites of civil society, the state and business (Chapters 4 to 6). Chapter 4 conceptualises civil society and reflects on its diversity and scales in degrowth transformations, paying attention to individuals and their self-transformation. Chapter 5 considers the state's roles in capitalist economies and its potential roles in degrowth transformations, bringing into focus various forms and scales of state intervention. Chapter 6 reflects on the role of business in degrowth transformations, addressing questions related to scale, diversity and business practices. Chapter 7 then provides an illustration of how a part of the book's theorisation of degrowth transformations can be applied empirically. The chapter relates data from empirical research on Sweden to the four planes of being, contemplating the potential uptake of degrowth ideas by different groups of people. Finally, in the Conclusion of the book, we synthesise the main arguments of the book, considering degrowth transformations in relation to the various planes of being and presenting our definition of degrowth. Further to this, we outline some key areas and focus points for future degrowth research and practice.

Notes

1 The notion that sustainability and growth can be reconciled can be seen, for instance, in the United Nations' 17 'sustainable development' goals. On one hand these concern, for instance, clean water, climate action, sustainable use of the seas and ecosystem protection, while on the other hand Goal 8 is to promote economic growth (UN 2015).
2 Only in the long run is capitalism itself in danger as a result of the climate breakdown. In the words of Malm (2018: 194), it is only likely to happen long after this breakdown 'has killed those at the greatest distance from the bourgeoisie'.
3 Many other strands within academia share degrowth advocates' desire of a good and harmonious life for all, including humans, nature and non-human beings. Such strands include diverse economies (Gibson-Graham and Dombroski 2020), deep ecology (Næss 2016), and scholarship on technological scepticism and pessimism (Heikkurinen and Ruuska 2021).

1

Capitalism, the growth imperative and (human) nature

Historically, humankind survived and advanced because humans lived in groups in which they learned to collaborate and divide tasks and in which they developed and used tools. This division of labour resulted in a differentiation of roles among members of society. In the earliest times, when productivity was low and members of society lived near the subsistence level, the differentiation was probably not very hierarchical. Yet as productivity increased with the innovation of ever more advanced technologies, it became possible for small classes of individuals to escape ordinary, physically hard labour and perform other societal functions. From this point onwards, hierarchical, class-based societies emerged and developed. These were societies in which members of lower classes performed the work needed to support all of society while members of higher classes – from slave owners in ancient Greece and Rome, over feudal lords in medieval Europe to capital owners in all capitalist societies – enjoyed the privilege of not being directly involved in the production of everyday necessities while still benefiting from them (Hunt 1975: 3–4).

In the present chapter we turn our attention towards capitalism. Doing so in a book on degrowth transformations is relevant insofar as the capitalist organisation of societies and the capitalist growth imperative are – as noted in the Introduction – root causes of the multidimensional crisis currently facing the earth and its inhabitants. As degrowth transformations cannot but start out from what currently exists, that is, capitalist societies, a holistic understanding of capitalism is a prerequisite for being able to theorise such transformations. By a holistic understanding we mean an understanding that takes into account capitalism's means of subsistence as well as effects on nature and human (and other) beings, instead of merely considering it narrowly as an economic system. In this context, we take up the question of whether egoism and greed are universally key human attributes. This issue is of key importance to any consideration of deep transformations, as deep social change beyond capitalism is only conceivable to the extent that human beings are able to change or manifest existing human qualities which transcend egoism and greed. Throughout the chapter we take selected ideas of Karl Marx as our point of departure, supplementing them with insights from a range of other social theorists along the way.

The growth imperative

Capitalism is a complex system of structures and other mechanisms, which is continuously transformed and reproduced through the activities of actors. The reproduction of the class structure through day-to-day working processes or the use of commodities and money through practices such as buying a cup of coffee is typically not the intended outcome of individual action (Koch 2020a). Unintended structural consequences follow from practices such as working and shopping because these phenomena are embedded in wider sets of, often unacknowledged, social structures, including the commodity form of work products, money and capital.

As countless scholars have observed, both in the degrowth literature and beyond, capitalism is structurally reliant on economic growth for its stability. For Marx, the origin of the imperative of capitalist economies to expand in scale and grow in value lies in the logic of exchange relations, especially the money form. He associated capitalism with endless M-C-M' cycles, where capital as money (M) is invested, then assumes commodify form (C), before it again assumes money form with added profits (M') (Marx 1990: 247–257). The amount of money invested in the beginning of the cycle (M) is transformed into a larger amount at the end of it (M') via wage labour using natural resources to produce commodities (C). Capital accumulation, then, depends on capital owners making profits by initiating the production of goods and services and subsequently being able to sell them (Jessop 2002).

Wage labour entails a commodification of work which occurs because employees have no alternative but to offer the only commodity at their disposal on 'labour markets'. Employees, in other words, exchange their capacity to work for a wage and are then forced to accept the right of their employer (the capital owner) to reap the profit (or absorb any losses) that results from the sale of the goods and services they have produced. Analysing the last step in the M-C-M' cycle, Marx (1990: 728) observes that there is 'not one single atom of its value that does not owe its existence to unpaid labour'. Further to this, the 'ownership of past unpaid labour is thenceforth the sole condition for the appropriation of living unpaid labour on a constantly increasing scale' (Marx 1990: 729).[1] Capitalism, then, is a system that is based on and produces deep inequalities.

The social structure of capitalism is complex and contradictory. Under feudalism, the vast majority of the population were bondmen and bond-women subject to direct legal and political domination by feudal lords.[2] Capitalism came to coexist with legal independence and political equality for citizens, including the right to be geographically mobile within the jurisdiction of the state. Citizens, including wage labourers, formally became politically and legally free to, for instance, vote and start a business. Nevertheless, they remained socially unequal in that most people found themselves having nothing to sell but their labour power while being separated from the means of subsistence such as land.[3] The production and reproduction of this inequality became one of the central questions for the social sciences from Marx onwards.[4] In addition to exploitation related to class differences, capitalism exhibits other, often intersecting (de los Reyes and Mulinari 2020), inequalities pertaining to, for example, gender, race and age.[5]

Capital accumulation generally unfolds in the context of corporate competition, that is, rivalry between firms for profits and market shares (on capitalist competition, see Buch-Hansen and Wigger 2011). In its most intense forms, competition 'strikes not at the margins of the profits and the outputs of the existing firms but at their foundations and their very lives' (Schumpeter 1947: 84). If they wish to survive, capitalist firms have no choice but to compete. The capital accumulation process, then, instils a grow-or-perish logic in the corporate sphere, as a result of which the interactions of capitalists can become like 'a fight among hostile brothers' (Marx 2006). Under this system, to avoid going out of business, companies seek to increase their productivity by being ever more efficient. As for capital owners, they are constantly watching out for investment opportunities that yield higher returns (extra profits) than those they get on their existing investments. In the words of Streeck (2016: 206), 'Social institutions that demarcate areas of trade against areas of non-trade, from national borders to laws prohibiting, say, the sale of organs, children, or cocaine, will find themselves under pressure from profit-pursuing actors seeking to extend economic exchange across demarcation lines.'

As a historical system, capitalism has been defined by making 'structurally central and primary the endless accumulation of capital' (Wallerstein 2000: 147). Certainly, other systems, including ancient civilisations and feudal societies, knew commitments to accumulation of wealth, especially the expansion of territory and riches earmarked for particular purposes such as the building of palaces or pyramids. Yet in such systems the pursuit of profit for its own sake tended to be seen as deviating from the norm. In medieval Europe, for example, economic interests tended to be subordinate to religion and the quest for 'salvation' (Weber 1958). Consequently, before the 1820s, when economic growth accelerated in the context of the Industrial

Revolution, economic activity around the world was characterised by periodic swings, yet expanded only by an average of 0.05% annually, due largely to slow population growth (Maddison 2001, 2007; see also Büchs and Koch 2017: chapter 2). In comparison, the annual average compound world growth rate was 2.21% from 1820 to 1998 (Maddison 2001: 28). Considering the nature of the capital accumulation process and the actual history of the capitalist economic system, there is little to suggest that a smaller and overall non-growing economy is potentially compatible with capitalism as a few scholars have suggested (e.g., Lawn 2011; for a critique of the suggestion, see, e.g., Spash 2020). By implication, far from being a process that can be reconciled with capitalism, degrowth points beyond and stands in opposition to it.

Work and consumption

In the chapter's introduction we noted how human beings have historically advanced as a species by dividing tasks. Marx (1875) viewed the division of labour as the necessary precondition for the 'all-round development of individuals' and their productive powers. Far from viewing economic growth as an ahistorical and quasi-eternal goal of economic action, he regarded economic expansion and a simultaneous intensification of the division of labour as a temporary and historically specific necessity to reach a development stage in which basic needs can be satisfied relatively easily, and where social actors are able to devote more time to purposes other than economic ones (Koch 2019a). He famously distinguished between the 'realm of freedom', which 'lies beyond the sphere of actual material production', and the 'realm of physical necessity' of material production, which can be temporarily reduced but not eliminated. Indeed, he was optimistic that the development of the productive forces under capitalism would create conditions making possible a reduction of the time devoted to material labour. Like many contemporary degrowth proponents, Marx viewed the shortening of the working day as the basic prerequisite for the realm of freedom to blossom (Marx 2006: chapter 48; see also Saito 2023: 238–239).

In capitalism, work is organised around the production of goods and services that the employer can sell with a profit, the very profit that allows capitalists to sustain and increase their powers. 'Workers', writes Harvey, are hereby 'put in a position where they can do nothing other than reproduce through their work the conditions of their own domination' (2014: 64). Work assumes the form of a paid activity that an individual performs in accordance with goals and procedures determined by the employer. The typical worker in capitalism, then, is an individual 'who produces nothing she or he consumes and consumes nothing he or she produces; for whom the essential objective of work is to earn enough to buy commodities produced and defined by the social machine as a whole' (Gorz 1989: 22). To the extent that the concrete work process of products is dominated by the valorisation process of capital, the employee is estranged or alienated (Marx 1977), not just from the products he or she contributes to producing, but also from nature, fellow humans and community. Alienation from nature can result from the work taking place in locations with a lack of access to nature, such as cities. It can also result from attributes of the workplace, the nature of the work itself and from long working hours that 'tie' the worker to the workplace.

Degrees of exposure to alienation vary with the position of the individual worker in the division of labour of a company. Ultimately it is a question of the extent 'to which involvement in one's work implies the enrichment or sacrificing of one's individual being. After my day's work, am I richer or poorer as a human being?' (Gorz 1989: 80). Though, potentially, work can be a source of fulfilment, personal growth and learning, a space where one's creativity can be exercised, the bulk of work under capitalism does not leave those who carry it out richer as human beings. The notion of alienation is therefore as relevant to the type of industrial work that was performed in the 'dark satanic mills' of the Industrial Revolution in Marx's lifetime, as it is to much work in contemporary capitalism. Cases in point include the work performed by today's global working class, most of which is located in developing and rising economies, and the widespread and growing existence in developed countries of 'bullshit jobs' (Graeber 2018), that is, jobs in, for example, financial services, administration, corporate law and public relations that are, according to the workers themselves, essentially meaningless and unnecessary.[6]

This brings us to the issue of the technology of work. As an economic system, capitalism is, on one hand, characterised by a 'strange stillness' in the form of the recurrent pattern of the M-C-M' cycle, a pattern which is repeated over and over again (Sewell 2008). On the other hand, there is flux. As a result of competition and the accumulate-or-perish logic, companies continuously reshape and innovate technologies, products and organisational forms to succeed in capitalist markets. The history of capitalism has thus been marked by deep changes in technologies and organisational forms – and these changes have, in turn, been accompanied by radical transformations of work. Much of the technological change that has happened over the course of capitalist history has been used to disempower and replace workers, in other words to the opposite of enriching their being (Harvey 2014: 270). Such transformations have been guided by what André Gorz referred to as economic rationality: the aspiration to use the factors of production, labour power included, as efficiently as possible to maximise profits. The economic rationalisation of work sweeps away 'the ancient idea of freedom and existential autonomy' and 'produces individuals who, being alienated in their work, will, necessarily, be alienated in their consumption as well and, eventually, in their needs' (Gorz 1989: 22).

As noted above, Marx (1977: 94) pointed to ownership of capital as the condition for accumulating more capital. He observed that

> private property has made us so stupid and one-sided that an object is only ours when we have it – when it exists for us as capital, or when it is directly possessed, eaten, drunk, worn, inhabited, etc., – in short, when it is used by us. ... In the place of all physical and mental senses there has therefore come the sheer estrangement of all these senses, the sense of having.

Building on these and other observations, German psychoanalyst Erich Fromm later developed an elaborate distinction between what he called the mode of having and the mode of being. The modes constitute two different ways of existence, two different orientations towards oneself and the world, which shape how a person thinks, feels and acts (2013: 21). The mode of having prevails under capitalism and is thus the mode we will focus on here – in later chapters we deal also with the mode of being. In the mode of having, a person's relationship to everything and anybody in the world is one of wanting to possess and own it/them. The relationship between the having person and what she owns is one of deadness: she has things because she has made them hers; but conversely things have her in the sense that her identity rests on what she has – money, stuff, prestige etc. – and what she consumes (2013: 21). Fromm notes that the most important form of having is consumerism and that the attitude inherent in it 'is that of swallowing the whole world' (2013: 24).

Pierre Bourdieu (1984) points to correspondence between individual consumption and positions in social space, especially class positions (see Koch 2019b). The cultural sphere is regarded as a site of symbolic struggles over the societal acceptability of lifestyles in which the dominant class manages to maintain a hierarchy of cultural forms that subjects all consumptive acts to the legitimate taste (its own). This process is objective and effective insofar as it operates largely independent of the (manipulative) intentions of dominant groups. While members of the middle and working classes may eschew legitimate cultural practices or regard them with suspicion and disdain, the position of the dominant class at the pinnacle of the cultural hierarchy normally goes unchallenged because it appears to be built upon ease, casualness and natural superiority. The competition for positional goods (Hirsch 1976) is mediated through a social logic referred to by Bourdieu (1984) as distinction, perceived as natural differences. The result of the naturalisation of the specifically capitalist character of production and consumption relations is that economic growth appears to be the ideal breeding ground for upward mobility and progress and in everyone's interest. With regard to production relations, a strong work ethic seems to be a worthwhile and rational individual strategy to 'get ahead', while in consumption, growth guarantees the creation of ever-new generations of consumer articles which are the material basis for individual distinction.

In capitalism, then, competition exists far beyond the marketplace. Fromm notes that a society revolving around profit and property produces a social character oriented around the having mode of existence, due to which key attributes of the relation between individuals are antagonism, competition and fear.

> If having is the basis of my sense of identity because 'I am what I have,' the wish to have must lead to the desire to have much, to have more, to have most. In other words, greed is the natural outcome of the having orientation. It can be the greed of the miser or the greed of the profit hunter or the greed of the womaniser or the man chaser. Whatever constitutes their greed, the greedy can never have enough, can never be satisfied.
>
> (Fromm 2013: 97)

Fromm observes that in capitalism, 'the having mode of existing is assumed to be rooted in human nature and, hence, virtually unchangeable' (2013: 86). This brings us to the question of human nature.

Human nature

The classical liberal creed asserts that human beings are innately egoistic, greedy, atomistic, coldly calculating, lazy and generally independent of society (Hunt 1975: 55). It is moreover assumed that it will benefit both the individual and society at large if such human beings are given the unrestrained freedom to compete in capitalist markets. In *The Wealth of Nations*, for example, Adam Smith (1976: 454) writes that

> every individual is continually exerting himself to find out the most advantageous employment for whatever capital he can command. It is his own advantage, indeed, and not that of the society, which he has in view. But the study of his own advantage naturally, or rather necessarily leads him to prefer that employment which is most advantageous to the society.

The notion that the actions of all humans flow from them being, in their essence, egoistic utility-maximisers has survived to this date, most notably in the *homo economicus* (economic man) of mainstream neoclassical economics.

Marx (1977, 1990) adopted a fundamentally different perspective, one involving a distinction between human nature in general and human nature as it is affected by a given type of society. As regards human nature in general, productive labour is held to be at the core of its essence. 'It is just in his work upon the objective world ... that man really proves himself to be a species-being. This production is his active species-life', writes Marx (1977: 69). Although other species are also productive, building nests and dwellings for themselves and their young, only human beings produce with tools. As a result, the productive powers of human beings – unlike the productive powers of other species – develop over time, and what is being produced takes a greater variety of forms than does the production of any other species. Moreover, only human beings produce even when they are free from the physical need to do so (1977: 68).

Seen from this perspective, human beings are not egoistic, greedy and competitive because their human nature dictates them to have such character traits; rather, the extent to which they are egoistic, greedy and competitive is a result of their character being moulded by the specific societal context in which they are situated. Instead of claiming that human beings are driven by egoism and the desire to maximise material gains, Marx claims that the way human beings produce in a specific spatio-temporal context has a decisive impact on his/her thinking and desires (Fromm 1961: 12). Consequently, being shaped by – and in turn contributing to shaping – the transformation of their natural and social environment, the concrete psychology of human beings will differ from one setting and one era to the next (Collier 2004: 25).

If engaging in productive labour is at the core of what defines human beings, it follows that the alienation of such labour under capitalism can only impact the inner being of humans in profound ways. In the words of Collier (2004: 25),

> the alienation of the human essence – productive labour – creates a totally different moral atmosphere from that, which, if Marx is correct, is natural to humankind. It makes people egoistic, not only in the sense that it sets everyone in mutual competition for survival, and thus corrupts our relations with our fellow humans, but also in the sense that it destroys our feel for the intrinsic value of things.

The commodification of labour under capitalism runs deeper than labour power itself being a commodity. It is not just that people come to experience themselves as commodities to be sold; it is also that, simultaneously, they have to act as the sellers of that commodity (Fromm 2013: 127). Because success depends on how well a person is able to sell him or herself in competitive labour markets, a decisive issue becomes how nice a 'personality package' that person is or can appear to be. That is, how reliable, robust, ambitious and so on he or she comes across. Offered for sale on the 'personality market', personality structures come to continuously adapt to the employer's desires and thus to exhibit great plasticity. Being saleable becomes the overriding concern of human beings. Associating this state of affairs with the having mode of existence, Fromm (2013: 86) notes that while humankind's biological urge for survival tends to further this mode, greed, selfishness and laziness 'are not the only propensities inherent in human beings'.[7]

As mentioned in the introduction to this chapter, the question of human nature is crucial when theorising degrowth transformations. Were capitalism a system existing in natural extension of an immutable human nature, deep transformations along the lines of degrowth would be ruled out. Fortunately, human nature is not fixed once and for all. Rather, as already noted, it is shaped by pre-existing social structures and cultures. Whereas capitalism produces 'as a chief incentive the desire for money and property', different 'economic conditions can produce exactly the opposite desires, like those of asceticism and contempt for earthly riches, as we find them in many Eastern cultures and in the early stages of capitalism' (Fromm 1961: 11). Under different socio-economic circumstances, then, greed and selfishness may become less prominent features of the personalities from which peoples' actions flow. In the words of Kallis et al. (2020: 42–43):

> To keep systemic expansion going, growth imperatives are internalized in life purposes and identities, making it feel like the impetus for growth is in our DNA. But ... [h]uman nature offers many possibilities: we can be selfish and we can be altruistic, we can want more and we can do well with less, we can accumulate but also share. Which propensities get cultivated and which ones constrained depends on sociocultural systems.

Further to this, it can also be noted that several degrowth scholars have referred to human needs theory (e.g., Büchs and Koch 2019). Such scholars, for instance, draw on Max-Neef's distinction between universal needs and culturally, socially and locally specific needs satisfiers (Max-Neef 1991; see also Chapters 5 and 7). This distinction draws attention to how, on one hand, human beings, qua their biological nature, universally have various needs in common and, on the other hand, to the specific spatio-temporal social conditions in which human lives are lived.

The capitalist consumerist culture incentivises people to work hard and long so as to be able to purchase commodities and commodified experiences. These commodities and experiences replace deeper, more enriching and lasting satisfactions (Soper 2020: 55). While human nature is shaped by consumer culture, it is not dictated by it. Human agency and inner being possess emergent properties making them irreducible to structures and discourses. A person can thus live in a capitalist consumer society without (entirely) internalising the prevailing culture of that society. Indeed, many people under capitalism live lives that are shaped by altogether different discourses, discourses that do not equate the 'good life' with consuming fashion items, air travel, cars, electronic goods, spacious accommodation and so forth. And there is growing realisation that the consumerist lifestyle is a source of over-work, depression and health problems (Soper 2020: 54). Even so, people in capitalist consumer societies are generally slow to change their lifestyles in 'a less energy-intensive and climate-adverse direction', both because they face many structural and cultural barriers such as the consumerist culture (Næss 2010: 69) and because the desire to have more is deeply ingrained in the social character (Fromm 2013).

In this and the preceding sections we have considered some key features of capitalism and some of the ways in which this economic system affects social life and the inner being of humans. As such, our perspective on capitalism so far has been an anthropocentric one. In the following section we broaden the perspective to situate capitalism in relation to the natural environment.

Capitalism and nature

Fundamentally opposing views as to the relationship between expanding capitalist market economies and the natural environment can be found in extant scholarship. Mainstream neoclassical economics regards the growth of monetary value as indefinite. Economic processes are conceptualised as if they were a closed system within which flows of services and goods are compensated by financial flows in the opposite direction. Energy, other natural resources and the earth in general are treated as if they were infinite and/or irrelevant. In this view, then, 'nothing enters from the environment, nothing exits to the environment. It does not matter how big the economy is relative to its environment' (Daly 1991: xiii). Yet economics has not always been synonymous with a science of prices, economic value and monetary growth. Political economists of the pre-industrial period did not conceive growth in abstract, quantifiable terms (Dale 2012a, 2012b) or as a key policy goal for governments.[8] Although Smith, David Ricardo and other classical economists pointed out that it is labour that produces exchange value, they did not go as far as to leave out nature from their analysis of economic processes (Koch 2012: 18).

For Marx, who witnessed a largely industrialised economy where most labour products had taken the form of commodities that were produced for the purpose of exchanging them on markets, labour is the connecting link between nature and human beings. In order to survive, humans must interact with nature and transform natural raw materials into use values. Building on Justus Liebig, Marx viewed this metabolism between human beings and nature through the labour process as an anthropological constant, as the 'everlasting nature-imposed condition of human existence' (Marx 1990). In this view, human life and society are embedded in and dependent on nature and the two are considered to exist in a dialectical relationship in which they continuously shape one another. In the words of Marx (1977: 67), 'That man's physical and spiritual life is linked to nature means simply that nature is linked to itself, for man is a part of nature.'

Under capitalism, the endless accumulation of capital is, as mentioned, made possible through the appropriation of unpaid labour or its product. Yet Marx (1990: 134) also observed, following William Petty, that 'labour is not the only source of material wealth, of use values produced by labour. ... labour is its father and the earth its mother'. To put it differently, the capital accumulation process is premised on production processes combining labour power with land, raw materials, fuels and the like. The C in the M-C-M' cycle, then, refers to commodity production processes that, in addition to creating increased exchange value, also involves the use and the destruction of nature. Gorz (1980: 20) notes that this destruction is inevitable: 'The earth is not naturally hospitable to humankind. Nature is not a garden planted for our benefit. Human life on earth is precarious and, in order to expand, it must displace some of the natural equilibriums of the ecosystem.' All human activities and social forms inevitably affect nature, but they can reshape it to smaller or larger extents and do so in more or less destructive ways. Capitalism is an extraordinarily destructive system, a system under which nature has been reshaped more than under any other system.[9]

Further to the above observations regarding the alienation of work and consumption under capitalism, Gorz (1989: 86) writes that 'learning to work means unlearning how to find, or even to look for, a meaning to non-instrumental relations with the surrounding environment and with other people'. In his analysis, the dominant culture in capitalism leads people to treat nature and fellow human beings in instrumental ways, doing violence to them. This violence is seen 'in the functionality both of our everyday tools and of the objects and spaces we have designed to support and contain our bodies: chairs, tables, furniture, streets, means of transport, urban landscapes, industrial architecture, noises, lights, materials and so on' (1989: 86). Again, it is important to recognise that there is a scale of violence. While some transactions with nature, such as fracking and large-scale conventional agriculture, are extremely violent, other transactions, such as small-scale organic agriculture, are hardly violent at all.

The logic of capital accumulation pushes companies to not only produce an ever-expanding range of commodities but also to invent ever-new wants that can be satisfied by means of these commodities. Historically, this process has resulted in (over)production divorced from basic or universal needs as defined by scholars such as Max-Neef or Doyal and Gough. And in parallel, it has resulted in the consumption of ever more nature. While the logic of capital accumulation reigns supreme, this process will not end until all of nature has been consumed. As an economic system, capitalism 'cannot help but privatise, commodify, monetise and commercialise all those aspects of nature that it possibly can. Only in this way can it increasingly absorb nature into itself to become a form of capital ... This metabolic relation necessarily expands and deepens in response to capital's exponential growth' (Harvey 2014: 262). Because it unfolds under the condition of competition which forces individual companies to speed up the overall turnover process as much as possible, the use and commercialisation of nature is continuously intensified and expanded, subsuming new geographical areas.

Though capitalist development cannot and does not get rid of the material and energy sides of production altogether, it nevertheless tends to negate and dispel them as much as possible (Burkett 1999). Whereas money and valorisation are quantitatively unlimited and, hence, reversible, natural resources are generally limited as the result of which the consumption of them is irreversible. The earth's stock of fossil fuels, in particular, is confined, and the existing stock can only be burnt once.[10] These contradictions and limits nevertheless place an expiry date on a growth-dependent economic system such as capitalism. When that date is depends on how successful capitalists are in pursuing their objectives: 'a way of life that bases itself on materialism, i.e. on permanent, limitless expansionism in a finite environment, cannot last long, ... its life expectation is the shorter the more successfully it pursues its expansionist objectives' (Schumacher 1993: 121). Still, capitalism exists, and, while it is not exactly thriving (see, e.g., Streeck 2016), it continues to overall grow five decades after Schumacher made this observation – and indeed after the Club of Rome published its *Limits to Growth* report (Meadows et al. 1972). While environmental limits to capital accumulation certainly exist, such limits will not by themselves bring an end to capitalism. Capital accumulation seems likely to continue well into the future, while the earth becomes increasingly uninhabitable for an ever-greater number of human and non-human beings.

Recognition of biophysical limits and the social and ecological downsides of endless growth led to the establishment of the field of ecological economics within heterodox economics. Pioneered by thinkers such as Georgescu-Roegen (1971), Herman Daly (1991) and Inge Røpke (2004), the field views economy and society as subsystems of nature. In the words of Clive Spash

(2020: 2), reality is 'a hierarchical structure with the economy emergent from and embedded in social relations, while social and economic systems are also subject to biophysical structures and their law like conditions'. In this view, capitalist growth some decades ago passed a point beyond which it became uneconomic in the sense that its social and ecological costs came to exceed the benefits of growth (Daly 1991). As mentioned above, ecological economics initially constituted the main scientific base for degrowth scholarship (Buch-Hansen and Nesterova 2021). It calls for limiting 'the physical scale of matter/energy throughput that sustains the economic activities of production and consumption of commodities' (Daly 1996: 31; see also Puller and Smith 2017).[11]

The notion of the Anthropocene has been used to describe a new geological era in which the activities of humankind have come to have a significant impact on the climate and ecosystem of the earth. While few deny that the activities of human beings have had and continue to have a massively negative impact on nature, the notion of the Anthropocene has been questioned for creating the appearance that the predicament we are now in is the unavoidable outcome of human biology or that it is an outcome for which all human beings are equally responsible. Yet some countries, classes and human beings are clearly more responsible for it than are others. In the words of Hornborg (2019: 141), 'the Anthropocene is the creation of a minority of the human species in its struggle to dominate and exploit the global majority'. The consequences for human beings of the violence and irreversible damage done to nature in the Anthropocene are also distributed unequally, with the severe overshooting of the earth's ecological boundaries having more fatal ramifications for 'those at the neo-colonised periphery' than for those 'in the neo-imperialising centres' (Soper 2020: 17). The fact that, historically, various modes of production have existed under which humanity did less violence to nature than has been the case under capitalism (Soper 2020) has led some to adopt the notion of Capitalocene (Moore 2017).

In conclusion: from capitalism in general to capitalism as a social formation

In the book's Introduction we noted that any social phenomenon exists simultaneously on four planes: material transactions with nature, social interactions between people/inter-subjectivities, social structure, and inner being. As shown in the present chapter, capitalism is no exception. Capitalism shapes humans' transactions with nature by exploiting, commodifying and transforming it into human artefacts at an ever-increasing rate. It alienates people from one another on the plane of social interactions. Its production relations hierarchise people on the plane of social structures. Finally, on the plane of inner being, capitalism brings out, nurtures and rewards greed and egoism, in combination with illusions of meritocracy. It promotes and normalises these traits, rendering opposition to capitalism more difficult.

In this chapter we have dealt with capitalism at a rather general level, for the most part at the level of what Marx called a 'mode of production', entailing for example that an abstraction is made from institutional regulation while individual actors are reduced to economic character masks (Marx 1990). Though the analysis of the mode of production allows for insights into the general tensions between economy, ecology and society that characterise all capitalist societies, it does not sufficiently consider how these structural tensions are articulated in actual societies and institutional circumstances.

For example, the long-term expansion of the scale of production and the associated increase in material and energy throughput under capitalism, and the ensuing rise of CO_2 emissions and the transgression of planetary limits, can be analysed at the level of abstraction of the mode of production. But such a perspective is too abstract and general to explain why CO_2 outputs per economic unit differ from one era to the next or why one capitalist country has considerably lower CO_2 outputs per capita than another (Fritz and Koch 2016). The tensions existing within the capitalist class in particular sectors also cannot be adequately analysed at the level of the mode of production. For example, whereas the profits of companies operating in some sectors may be negatively affected by specific forms of environmental protection, companies in other sectors may benefit from it (Görg 2003: 286). And whereas for most entrepreneurs the overconsumption of raw materials and natural resources is a means of valorisation, for others it threatens profitability. When, for example, the rainforest is cut down, it places strain on resources required by the pharmaceutical industry (Dietz and Wissen 2009).

Actual capitalist economies and societies, that is, capitalist *social formations* (Poulantzas 1968), are far more complex than capitalism viewed as a mode of production. They are dominated by this mode yet also feature elements of non-capitalist economies, corresponding forms of domination and a range of real-type combinations of productive and unproductive as well as paid and unpaid work contexts (Gibson-Graham 2006; Koch 2011).[12] And over time social formations change profoundly (Buch-Hansen 2014; Lipietz 1992). In other words, it should be recognised that not only do different, coexisting and competing forms of capitalism exist, but also that capitalism as an economic system is not all-pervasive. In each of the four planes capitalist manifestations coexist with non-capitalist ones (Buch-Hansen and Nesterova 2023). Proceeding along these lines, that is, taking into consideration diversity within and beyond capitalism, the following chapters add nuance to the perspective presented in this chapter.

Notes

1 The transfer of surplus labour is hidden through the continuing distortion of specifically capitalist economic categories and social relations into objects and natural features (Koch 2018a). Consequently, while capitalism is premised on the exploitation of employees, it comes to appear as if all labour is paid and as if profit derives from other sources than surplus labour.

2 Bondmen and -women were part of the personal possession of their feudal lords, just as the land or the tools used in agriculture. They were tied to the place where they worked and could not move without the consent of their landlords. Both were politically and legally unequal.

3 Marx (1990: chapter 24) described the historical separation process of labour and land using the example of the Scottish Highland Clearances. This case of 'enclosing the commons' gave later rise to the formulation of the general concept of 'accumulation by dispossession' (Luxemburg 1951; Harvey 2005), which was applied to processes of corporatisation, privatisation and commodification of previously public assets, from water and public utilities to social housing and academia.

4 This tension between the spheres of production and circulation made Marx regard capitalism as a historical transition period. The experiences of equality, individual independence and mutual respect, associated with the circulation of commodities, awaken and increase the will and the potential in humans to also make these core characteristics of their work relations and hence a post-capitalist mode of production.

5 The latter are forms of 'exclusion', denoting a situation in which the material benefits of one group are acquired at the expense of another group, coercive practices being an essential part of the process. 'Exploitation' is a specific form of exclusion in that the 'material well-being of exploiters depends on the effort of the exploited' (Wright 1994: 40), whereas in non-exploitative exclusion there is no labour transfer from the excluded to the excluding group. The crucial difference is that in the former case, the exploiter needs the exploited, whereas in the latter case the excluding group is sometimes better off if the excluded group simply disappeared (Koch 2017: chapter 1).

6 Schumacher (1993: 39–40), arguing for a Buddhist economics, noted how organising 'work in such a manner that it becomes meaningless, boring, stultifying, or nerve-racking for the worker would be little short of criminal: it would indicate a greater concern with goods than with people, an evil lack of compassion and a soul-destroying degree of attachment to the most primitive side of this worldly existence'.

7 The philosopher Baruch Spinoza thought of greed and ambition not as natural aspects of human nature but as mental illnesses. In *Ethics* (1677) he makes the following observation: 'if the greedy person thinks only of money and possessions, the ambitious one only of fame, one does not think of them as being insane, but only as annoying; generally one has contempt for them. But factually, greediness, ambition, and so forth are forms of insanity, although usually one does not think of them as "illness" ' (cited in Fromm 2013: 82).

8 This changed in the course of the nineteenth century, when use values, matter and energy were reduced to abstract numbers and monetary magnitudes started to become a salient feature of economic life. In the first half of the twentieth century, this development reached a new level when, in 1932, the US Congress commissioned the economist Simon Kuznets to devise a means by which to measure the nation's output. This resulted in the Gross National Product (GNP) and later the Gross Domestic Product (GDP), a measure that estimated the market value of all final goods and services produced within a country per year, including the costs of government services (Paulsson 2019). Subsequently, not least in the post-Second World War period, GDP growth became a dominant priority for all countries, informing practices and policies that have deeply shaped societies and the planet (Schmelzer 2016).

9 This is, of course, not to suggest that capitalism is the only environmentally unsustainable type of economic system. Most notably, Soviet communist countries were fossil fuel-based economies that strove for high economic growth rates. As a result, their ecological footprints were very large.

10 Hornborg (2019: 17) speaks of 'modernity as a social condition founded on the capacity to externalize biophysical burdens and risks'.

11 While it is, as such, not first and foremost preoccupied with GDP growth, limiting the scale of matter/energy throughput to a level where the economy works within ecological boundaries would undoubtedly result also in a smaller GDP.

12 If we do not consider the fact that capitalism proceeds in different growth strategies and modes of regulation, then we run the risk of repeating the errors of earlier generations of Marxists who thought that the social tensions and contradictions inherent in capitalism as mode of production would lead to its inevitable and in some cases immediate collapse.

2

Institutional forms and diversity: from capitalism to degrowth

The capital accumulation process is pervaded by several tensions and contradictions that manifest as continuous features of, or ruptures in, the development of capitalism (Harvey 2014). Due to its contradictory nature, capitalism depends on the existence of societal institutions beyond the market to temporarily stabilise it (Jessop 2002: 19). Various strands of scholarship deal with this phenomenon.[1] In this chapter, we build upon regulation theory, which was designed to consider the specific social, cultural and institutional forms and frameworks within which capitalist growth in actual social formations proceeds. According to this theory, accumulation regimes need to be stabilised by modes of regulation conceptualised in terms of various institutional forms: the wage–labour nexus, the enterprise form, the monetary regime, the state and insertion into international regimes (Boyer and Saillard 2002; Koch 2012; Lipietz 1992). In addition to this, regulationist scholarship has dealt with the relation to nature of specific accumulation regimes.

Consideration of institutional forms has so far predominantly entered analyses of capitalist social formations. Degrowth scholarship has not, for the most part, adopted the concept, or for that matter regulation theory terminology more generally (but see Koch and Buch-Hansen 2021). It is thus safe to say that comprehensive answers as to what the various institutional forms could involve in relation to degrowth (that is, whether they could come to stabilise a degrowth economy) have not been provided. Nevertheless, to varying extents, ideas or visions related to each form have been developed, both by degrowth scholars and scholars working on, for instance, eco-feminism and diverse economies. In this chapter we relate to some of these ideas to contemplate what transformations towards degrowth could entail. Moreover, we bring up the issue of what capitalist diversity means for such transformations. First, however, we consider institutional forms under capitalism.

Institutional forms

The concept of institutional forms refers to the various institutional arrangements that, in a given spatio-temporal setting, lend stability to a specific regime of accumulation (Piletic 2019: 1310). By implication, institutional forms vary in place and time. The examples of Fordist and neoliberal capitalism can be used to exemplify this point. The Fordist era in the decades after the Second World War is often referred to as the Golden Age of Capitalism (e.g., Glyn et al. 1990). It entailed 'a virtuous circle of growth based on mass production, rising productivity based on economics of scale, rising incomes linked to productivity, increased mass demand due to rising wages, increased profits based on full utilization of capacity and increased investment in improved mass production equipment and techniques' (Jessop 2002: 56). Overall, institutional forms in this era delivered stable accumulation and social progress in the advanced capitalist countries for approximately three decades (Neilson 2020).

The content of the institutional forms in the Fordist mode of regulation was characterised by the following features. Its *wage–labour nexus* involved industrial relations systems with minimum wage levels and generalised collective agreements that coupled wages and productivity increases. Its *enterprise form* involved large corporations oriented towards economies of scale production and an oligopolistic form of competition. Its *monetary regime* entailed credit money and credit policies oriented towards maintaining aggregate demand in national markets. In terms of *state form*, a Keynesian welfare state provided social security for citizens, ensuring that they remained consumers even in the absence of employment. And, finally, the *international system* was oriented towards the expansion of trade and investment in the Atlantic zone (Jessop 2002: 57; Boyer and Saillard 2002; Lipietz 1992). Of these institutional forms, the wage–labour nexus prevailed in the Fordist mode of regulation: 'The necessity of a parallel evolution of mass consumption and mass production for the coherence of Fordism put the institutional arrangements of the wage–labour nexus at the centre of the whole institutional architecture' (Amable 2000: 665). As this indicates, not only does the content of the various institutional forms vary, so does their internal hierarchy, which is to say that one or more institutional forms matter more than the rest in a given mode of regulation.

After the 1970s, Fordist-Keynesian capitalism gave way to a postfordist-neoliberal form of capitalism (henceforth denoted neoliberal capitalism). In Chapter 3 we consider some of the mechanisms causing this shift. In the present context we can note that the new form of capitalism entailed deep changes in all the institutional forms making up the previously existing modes of regulation. Neoliberal capitalism involves a finance-dominated accumulation regime, and a key feature of its mode of regulation is financial deregulation (Skyrman 2022; see also Koch 2012: 87). Entailing deregulation of domestic financial systems combined with the liberalisation of international capital flows, financial deregulation fundamentally changed the financial landscape and enhanced the power of the financial sector (Stockhammer 2011: 239). The growing weight of finance in the economy is often referred to as financialisation (Krippner 2005). As observed by Frieden (2007: 385), 'By the late 1990s international financial activities were so intertwined with domestic financial markets that for all intents and purposes there was one global financial system that included all the developed countries and many developing and formerly Communist countries.' In terms of the hierarchy of institutional forms, regulation theorists have suggested that this *monetary regime* is at the top under neoliberal capitalism (e.g., Boyer and Saillard 2002; Piletic 2019).

It is not so much the transnationalisation of finance, however, as the transnationalisation (globalisation) of the production process that qualitatively sets the neoliberal era apart from previous eras (Robinson 2004). This development was closely related to gigantic, transnational corporations (TNCs) becoming the dominant *enterprise form*. The number of such corporations increased from approximately 7,000 in 1970 to over 38,000 in 1995 and to more than 100,000 in 2010 (Jaworek and Kuzel 2015; Robinson 2004: 55–56). Paralleling this development was a massive increase in foreign direct investment (FDI) – that is, investments that are made to acquire interests in companies operating outside the economy of the investor. In the neoliberal era, deindustrialisation, technological change and the growing transnationalisation of ownership structures and production circuits marked a gradual and partial transition towards a more flexible type of capitalism (Jessop 2002). The transnationalisation of economic structures intensified competitive pressures and forced many companies to become more flexible.

This development translated, for instance, into a push for more flexible labour markets, resulting in a move away from the existing *wage–labour nexus*. 'The developed economies needed to adjust to a new and emerging division of labour, where huge differences in unit labour costs stimulated the relocation of production especially in manufacturing' (Dannreuther and Petit 2006: 106). As a result, wages and social protection came under pressure in the advanced capitalist countries. This development was to no small extent driven by changes in the *state form*. Keynesian welfare states were gradually transformed into competition states. These expose citizens to the forces of competition and promote social solidarity only insofar as it constitutes an asset in global competition (Cerny 1997; Hirvilammi and Koch 2020; Streeck 2000). In parallel, state regulation of the economy in a broad range of areas was 'neoliberalised', the areas of competition policy, industrial policy and monetary policy being cases in point (e.g., Buch-Hansen and Wigger 2011; Bulfone 2022). This development was to no small extent due to the emergence in the *international* system of loose networks made up of trans- and supranational organisations such as the OECD, IMF, WTO, World Bank and EU, together with national states. These networks, which can also be thought of as transnational state apparatuses (Robinson 2004), serve to organise the conditions of transnational accumulation. In this transnational architecture, states compete with one another to attract mobile capital.

A sixth institutional form? The social relation to nature

Different accumulation regimes correspond to specific forms of appropriation of nature by society. For example, accumulation regimes may be linked to specific forms of energy consumption such as biotic, fossil and renewable energy sources. This is reflected in regulation theory, where some scholars speak of 'energy regimes' or more broadly 'the social relation to the environment'. There is some disagreement among regulation theorists as to whether the social relation to the environment constitutes an institutional form in its own right. Some argue that the relation to the environment is governed by all the fundamental social relations of capitalism, as a result of which it does not constitute an institutional form in its own right (Douai and Montalban 2012). Others argue that it is meaningful to consider the relation to the environment as a sixth institutional form inasmuch as the specific manner in which energy/matter is utilised is subject to regulation (Becker and Raza 2000). This institutional form, then, regulates 'access to, and utilization of, the material world both for productive and reproductive activities. Hence, it also regulates the spatial and temporal distribution of the ecological costs and benefits of these (re-)productive activities' (2000: 10). Synthesising these perspectives, Cahen-Fourot (2020) proposes that while each of the five traditional institutional forms is likely to influence society–nature relations, the combination of all their effects is what produces a particular relation between the mode of regulation and the environment.

Here we proceed on the assumption that the social relation to the environment can meaningfully be considered a distinct institutional form, yet consistent with the terminology used in Chapter 1, we refer to it as the *social relation to nature*. Considering this institutional form first in relation to

Fordist capitalism, we can note that this type of capitalism delivered some decades of economic growth and social progress in the advanced capitalist countries. It did so, in processes mediated by global value chains, on the basis of highly violent social relations to nature (Brand and Wissen 2012). That is, the aforementioned Golden Age of Capitalism in the Global North was premised on massive consumption of fossil energy and only possible due to the overexploitation of natural resources. Had all people led lifestyles corresponding to what many Westerners came to think of as adequate mate- rial welfare levels after the Second World War, the planet would have ended in an acute climate emergency significantly earlier (Koch and Mont 2016; Fritz and Koch 2016). Fordist progress, then, was accompanied by massive growth in CO_2 emissions. Indeed, the origins and development of the global climate crisis relate directly to 'the upswing and generalisation of the Fordist production and consumption norm in the Western world and of the simulta- neous establishment of an international division of labour in industrialised and extraction societies' (Koch 2012: 83; see also Lessenich 2019). For this and other reasons (Laruffa 2022: 124), Fordism and the Keynesian welfare state should not be glamorised.

As for neoliberal capitalism, it certainly inflicts no less violence on nature than did its predecessor. Aside from remaining overwhelmingly reli- ant on fossil fuels, an inbuilt problem of neoliberal capitalism is that with the weakening of labour, wages and thus aggregate demand levels in the advanced capitalist countries came under pressure (e.g., Kotz 2010). This inbuilt problem was dealt with partly by maintaining and even increasing levels of private consumption by facilitating the increased indebtedness of households, partly by exporting the Western consumption norm to other parts of the world. The result is that 'at no other point in time have so many people in the world participated in consumption patterns that used to be the privilege of elites' (Koch 2012: 120). Under neoliberal capitalism, then, despite greener technologies, more natural resources are being used than ever before – with the distribution of this use and extraction being massively unequal (e.g., Soper 2020: 39; see also Neilson 2020). The violent extrac- tion of natural resources continues, mainly in the Global South. Yet it is also important to recognise that it occurs within countries in the Global North. For example, peripheral regions of Finland have 'been one of the key tar- gets of the recent global boom in the quest for untapped mineral resources' (Lassila 2018: 1).

As noted above, the social relation to nature in a given social formation will be influenced by other institutional forms. The state form is a case in point. Some scholars speak of the emergence of a green or environmental state in the last third of the twentieth century (Eckersley 2004; Hausknost 2020; Koch 2020b). Just as the welfare state emerged together with the institutionalisation of the wage–labour nexus to mediate capital–labour relations and to limit the social damages caused by capitalist production, so the environmental state serves to limit, to a certain extent, the environmental damages caused by capitalist accumulation (Gough 2016). Similarly, the structures of the international system have a major impact on social relations to nature in every country. For example, patterns of resource extraction are shaped by free trade legislation enforced by international organisations.

In the context of degrowth social formations, the social relation to nature would be altogether different from how such relations are and have been in different capitalist social formations. Transactions with nature would be characterised less by violence and more by gentleness and care (Buch-Hansen and Nesterova 2023). In capitalist social formations, nature is regarded as a pile of resources that can be extracted, monetised, exchanged and consumed. Nature, then, is valuable because it is a source of raw materials and energy that humans can use. Degrowth, conversely, views nature, including non-humans, as inherently valuable irrespective of their usefulness for humans. In economic and social practice, gentleness and care towards nature would involve both reduction and growth in different domains. An overall far smaller throughput of matter and energy necessitates growth in nature- and place-based economic activities as well as more sufficiency-based modes of being. A major reduction of fossil fuel use requires growth in renewable and localised energy production. Importantly, there are limits as to how localised such production can meaningfully become, especially in the short run. Equipment such as wind turbines, solar panels and the like typically requires long supply chains, which are themselves associated with high energy consumption. Existing localised production of renewable energy, for example using wood as biofuel, is not necessarily more sustainable than production requiring long supply chains. Considered as a distinct institutional form, gentle social relations to nature would be placed high in the hierarchy of such forms in degrowth social formations. In other words, it would have a deep impact on the functioning of the other institutional forms.

This consideration brings us to the more general matter of what degrowth could entail in relation to the remaining institutional forms. Being an anti- and post-capitalist project, it is clear that institutional forms under degrowth would not serve to stabilise capital accumulation. Instead, they would be oriented towards facilitating gentle social relations to nature as well as social equity to ensure satisfaction of the basic needs of humanity now and in the future. It is an open question whether the same institutional forms – the wage–labour nexus, the enterprise form, the monetary regime, the state form and insertion into international regimes – would also be the key forms in the post-capitalist context of degrowth. In the following, we will assume that they would (in versions profoundly different from their current manifestations) and bring together ideas and visions from degrowth scholarship and related literatures that more or less closely connect to each form. The purpose of this exercise is not to present a blueprint of institutional forms under degrowth. Providing such a blueprint would be meaningless, both because the future is not predetermined and because institutional forms under degrowth would neither be uniform across space nor be fixed once and for all. Rather, the purpose is to think, at a general level, about what degrowth could entail in various interrelated dimensions and in this context indicate the depth of the transformations it would require. While touching upon all the institutional forms in the following sections, we devote most attention to the wage–labour nexus and money, as later chapters deal in greater depth with the remaining forms.

The wage–labour nexus

Several growth-critical scholars have observed how, under capitalism, work is intimately entangled with the growth imperative. Jackson and Victor (2011) speak of a productivity trap, which involves companies, in order to increase profits and market shares, seeking to grow labour productivity. As a result, fewer employees are needed to produce the same quantity of goods and services, meaning that unemployment increases in the absence of economic growth. For those affected, unemployment entails a loss of meaning, identity, social status and the ability to consume. The trap, then, contributes to creating widespread support for economic growth. While not necessarily involving the abandonment of wage labour, degrowth would involve breaking with productivity growth and entail various transformations of work. Barca (2019), for example, advocates a liberation from and of work. The *liberation from work* involves a reduction in work time and the simultaneous creation of time and spaces beyond work-life for regenerative activities, community building and activism. The introduction of a universal basic income is a policy that could contribute towards this end. The *liberation of work* involves changing the predominant nature of work, for instance in terms of how it is controlled, organised and distributed. This could entail that work is increasingly controlled by those carrying it out, that work is organised more democratically and less hierarchically, and that both stimulating work and less pleasant but necessary work is distributed more equally (see also Chertkovskaya and Paulsson 2021).

Wage labour is the predominant form taken by work under capitalism, yet zooming in on existing societies it can be seen that labour, including wage labour, takes multiple forms. Diverse economies scholarship brings into focus this diversity (e.g., Gibson-Graham and Dombroski 2020).

It notes that some labour is unpaid, including labour undertaken by non-human species, housework, family care, emotional labour, neighbourhood work, volunteering and slave labour. As for waged work, it also takes a variety of forms, ranging from salaried and unionised work to increasingly common precarious forms of work, such as part-time, non-unionised, temporary, freelance and seasonal work. Finally, several forms of work that are remunerated in ways other than with wages exist, including, for example, self-employed, self-provisioning, cooperative, indentured, feudal, reciprocal and bartered labour (Gibson-Graham and Dombroski 2020: 13).

It is in non-profit-oriented work contexts that niches relevant for degrowth transformations are most likely to be developed and expanded (Hinton 2020). Feminist scholars have long noted that work of essential importance to the functioning of society either does not take the form of wage labour or is underpaid and under-recognised. Most notably, reproductive care work – taking care of children and elderly and various household work – is mainly undertaken by women and is not regarded as proper work. In the Global North, where many women work in the wage-labour market, much care work has been commodified, for example by being outsourced to privatised care providers employing underpaid, mainly female, caregivers from the Global South (Dengler and Seebacher 2019). Feminist degrowth scholars envision gender-just care beyond monetary valuation (Dengler and Lang 2022). They note that the reorganisation of care needs to take into consideration the diversity of currently existing care arrangements existing around the globe and that 'many of today's examples for caring commons are found in the Global South, where communitarian caring commons ... and more generally, communal modes of living have survived colonial intrusion at the margins of capitalism' (2022: 17). It is important to add to this that in many places communal modes of living come with family obligations, arranged marriages, traditional gender roles and restricted freedoms, especially for women. As such, these communities should not be romanticised in general. Also, for the sake of nuance, it is important to recognise that not only women perform underpaid, under-recognised and undesirable work: for example, many dirty industries with dangerous work employ mainly male workers. For degrowth, then, the point is not just to emancipate women but to emancipate humanity (see also Bhaskar 2012a).

As noted in the Introduction, degrowth as we understand it involves massive growth in some sectors such as organic agriculture and renewable energy, combined with the shrinkage or abolition of other sectors. These other sectors include polluting sectors such as oil and coal, sectors promoting unsustainable consumption such as advertising, sectors manufacturing products that inflict harm on people and nature such as the military industry, and sectors creating little use value, finance being a case in point.

By implication, the distribution of jobs across sectors – and thus the prevalent nature of work – would be very different in the context of degrowth. Under degrowth, the bulk of employment would have to be shifted from jobs that are environmentally harmful to jobs that entail gentler relations to nature. An aspect of such gentleness relates to the types of outputs resulting from work. Desirable outputs are goods and services that directly benefit nature (for example, composting food waste) or constitute ecologically generalisable need satisfiers (for example, organic horticulture providing people with food). Conversely, undesirable outputs are ones entailing unnecessary violence done to nature. Cases in point are work outputs designed to satisfy luxury wants for, say, holidays in distant locations, SUVs and villas (Bohnenberger 2022). Another sustainability-related aspect of work concerns lifestyles. A sustainable work-lifestyle exists when a job does not prevent the employee and his or her household from leading a sustainable lifestyle. A job can do so in various ways. It can, for instance, provide income that is too low for the employee to be able to make sustainable choices, such as buying organic food. Conversely, a job can provide income that is so large that it enables the employee to lead a grossly unsustainable lifestyle (Bohnenberger 2022).[2]

In the previous chapter we noted how, in capitalism, most jobs alienate workers. Moreover, many jobs result in employees suffering from burnout and stress. Degrowth advocates envision a post-capitalist society in which the pace is slower, including in the area of work. Soper (2020) imagines a society in which state-of-the-art technologies in the energy and medical areas blend with the reinstatement of previous ways of producing and providing. Specifically, she has in mind the expansion of craft ways of working with 'their emphasis on skill, attention to detail, and personal involvement and control' (Soper 2020: 100). The use of skill, the exercise of mental concentration and the satisfaction it can give rise to means that such work has relevance in post-capitalist contexts. Soper underscores the importance of not reproducing the exploitative nature of labour processes associated with artisan work in premodern times, of cutting the link between economic growth and progress without dismissing 'the advances in democracy and social and sexual emancipation that have accompanied the development of market society and mass production' (2020: 104).

The monetary regime

As noted above, a monetary regime characterised by deregulated financial systems and liberalised international capital flows is at the top of the hierarchy of institutional forms in neoliberal capitalism. More generally, the nature of money and the financial system is at the core of what makes possible the commodification of nature and social life under capitalism, leading to a variety of ills. The current international financial system, for example, facilitates the drain of natural resources from the Global South to the Global North due to debt relations and financial dependency (Dziwok and Jäger 2021). Money is unlikely to disappear in a degrowth society, yet in the literature on degrowth, various proposals are discussed that involve money coming to play a different and overall far less prominent role. In other words, the monetary regime would be placed much lower in the hierarchy of institutional forms than is the case under neoliberal capitalism.

A demonetisation of pursuits such as food and energy production is a key way in which money could become less important in degrowth social formations. That is, to the extent people can use or share energy and food they themselves have contributed to producing, these activities come to exist outside the capitalist accumulation process and thus no longer translate into economic growth (Heikkurinen et al. 2019). Demonetising these and other pursuits could not only result in all basic human needs being satisfied outside the framework of capitalism, it could also free time and energy for other activities, such as activism and education. This would mark a shift in relation to (neoliberal) capitalism where, as previously noted, much such time and energy is tied to wage labour. The use of time banks, where time is the unit of currency, is a means through which demonetisation can unfold. Other practices of demonetisation could be barter (Trainer 2012) and the introduction of local currencies (Dittmer 2013). Demonetisation, then, is a process that would result in the shrinking of the space in which monetised relations and the accumulate-or-perish logic of capitalism prevail.

Another proposal discussed in the literature on degrowth is to put the creation of money under public control, so as to democratise the monetary regime and increase the probability that money is provided for societally desirable purposes (Cahen-Fourot et al. 2022: 344). Investments would, for instance, be channelled to sustainable, non-growing businesses, community energy initiatives, and improvements of public infrastructure and transport, as well as worker-led organisations (Chertkovskaya and Paulsson 2021: 417). This would require legislation at the national and international levels, legislation requiring public banks to serve the common good by providing money for activities satisfying human needs (as opposed to wants) and gentler relations to nature.

In recent years there has been much talk of green finance in degrowth circles and beyond. Originating in financial-sector strategies, green finance initiatives for the most part serve mainly to turn the climate and biodiversity crises into profit opportunities for the sector. Such initiatives, then, are reformist in nature and do not point beyond capitalism. Yet other visions of green finance are more progressive. Distinguishing between different varieties of green finance and monetary policy, Dziwok and Jäger (2021) identify a variety which they consider broadly compatible with degrowth. They call, for instance, for the expansion and transformation of so-called debt-for-nature swaps. Such swaps involve forgiving foreign debt obligations, allowing debtor nations to use the money for environmental purposes. They also suggest that monetary policy can provide a global institutional setting within which resources for the attainment of global sustainable welfare can be provided (Dziwok and Jäger 2021). For green finance to become compatible with degrowth, the financial sector would need to give up its one-sided fixation on growth and focus instead on the common good and relocate vast sums of finance to other areas (Dörry and Schulz 2022). That is, in contemporary capitalism, money is channelled to where returns on investment are high or acceptable. In degrowth social formations, the point would be to channel money to where ecological and social returns are high, that is, where it is needed, irrespective of the potential return. For instance, this may include financing small-scale businesses which do not plan to grow and pursue sufficiency in the size or scale of the business.

Currently a lot of so-called green finance is channelled to activities aiming to lower carbon emissions, such as renewable energy. The main struggle small, non-growth-oriented sustainable companies are currently facing is a lack of access to finance. Under degrowth, financing would not depend on businesses wanting to grow (Nesterova 2021a). Seen from the perspective of degrowth, this focus is inadequate as it risks forgoing support towards other transformative forms of business. Cases in point could be local craft and artisanal businesses, small-scale organic farmers, repair cafés, libraries, renting services, lower and appropriate technologies, businesses that produce durable products, and alternative, affordable dwellings. If so-called green finance is to make a difference in degrowth transformations, the meaning of 'green' needs to be redefined and expanded, to concern not just low carbon but to also include other degrowth-compatible businesses and initiatives.

Under normal (capitalist) circumstances, little investment which does not promise return would be happening. To avoid such an outcome in degrowth social formations, the state would in all likelihood need to oversee financing and change the terms on which it takes place. One aspect could be to prevent investment in undesirable industries while facilitating resources being channelled towards genuinely green industries. Another aspect could be to provide financing without interest repayment. Such financing would reduce pressures on businesses – including pressures to grow because of borrowing necessitating repayment with interest. In contemporary capitalism, innovative businesses experimenting with local materials and new business models particularly struggle to obtain funding as they are often perceived as risky.

Green finance (as understood here) without interest could help such businesses and encourage more people to perhaps seek and try such employment rather than employment in 'bullshit jobs' in inhumane multinational corporations. A third aspect of the role the state could play in facilitating (genuine) green finance concerns the principles of financing. Many people feel powerless in relation to the current financial system. They are confronted with certain rules of the game which they are required to accept as something given. For example, if they want to start a business, they have to promise growth to the financing institution, borrow, repay with interest or even adjust their business plan (which may go against their original idea) in order to be granted a loan. Changing these rules of the game, the state could pave the way for different principles of financing, making it more accessible to a wider range of people and purposes.

In thinking about money, it is important to recognise that it is not a homogeneous artefact. Hornborg (2019) distinguishes the currently prevailing form of general-purpose money from special-purpose money. General-purpose money is underpinned by the notion that anything can be converted into anything else. Child labour can be bought for money deriving from the sale of wine gums or guns. 'In making all values interchangeable', Hornborg (2019: 6–7) writes, 'general purpose money dissolves the kinds of distinctions on which all living systems depend: between the short term and the long term, the small scale and the large scale, the trivial and the essential'. The problem with this form of money is that there are no constraints on what can be bought for it. Consumers, then, are incentivised to search for the best deal and use the money to purchase the least expensive products available. That these products are cheap is often a function of how they were produced in the first place, that is, with little regard for the wellbeing of employees and nature. Hornborg envisions a reform of the currency system which leads to the introduction of a digital, special-purpose currency that exists next to general-purpose money. This complementary currency, which is to be introduced in each country and be distributed to all its citizens as a basic income, can be used only for local use. That is, the currency can only be used for purchasing goods and services produced within a certain geographical radius of the location of the purchase. Key purposes of such a currency are to limit the damage done by transnational financial speculation and reduce long-distance transportation of goods and the associated harm done to nature, while increasing local cooperation and integration (Hornborg 2019: 233–242).

Hornborg's proposal is appealing but not without challenges. While local production may sound, and is often presented as, desirable, it is important to be aware that such production (if at all possible) may itself conceal long supply chains. That is, as also touched upon above, a locally made product may still require equipment and ingredients made elsewhere, equipment and ingredients that may themselves be products requiring long supply chains. Even locally grown food requires the use of equipment and machines (if not the chemicals, packaging or energy) made outside the location where it is grown. If, then, consumers are to be able to make informed decisions with respect to the purchase of products which are eligible for being bought with special-purpose currencies, full disclosure of what went into the production of these products would be necessary. Another noteworthy consideration is the digital nature of special-purpose currency. While in the minds of the public the currency may be geographically restricted, enabling its use is far less geographically limited. For instance, data centres which make data storage possible may be located elsewhere. Digital currencies also require digital/electronic devices which likewise necessitate long supply chains. This is not to discount the potential value of special-purpose currencies, but rather to highlight that reduction in, for example, long-distance transportation in one domain does not necessarily eliminate the issue of long-distance transportation altogether.

The state, the international system and business

The state in capitalist social formations is, unsurprisingly, a *capitalist* state. That is, it is a state that in various ways serves to facilitate the capital accumulation process. It does this in a variety of ways, which differ from one formation to another. In neoliberal capitalism, which primarily serves the interests of transnational capital, a key function of the state and international organisations is to serve as promoters of competition both in the corporate sphere and in society at large. Owing to a deep suspicion of democracy, key state institutions, such as central banks, are insulated from democratic pressures (Buch-Hansen and Wigger 2011; Harvey 2005). Moreover, even when it assumes the guise of an 'environmental state' that reduces the damage caused to nature by the working of capitalism, the social relation to nature remains a grossly violent one.

For degrowth social formations to work, a very different type of state would be needed. For one thing, the orientation of the 'degrowth state' would be profoundly different from that of the neoliberal capitalist state. In degrowth social formations, state interventions at all scales (local, national, transnational) would promote gentle social relations to nature and human needs satisfaction for all. This would be reflected in how tax revenues are used, namely on sustainable welfare (see Chapter 5), universal basic income and universal basic services rather than on, say, the military complex and subsidies for dirty industries. The degrowth state would heavily tax polluters and income and/or wealth above a certain level and use these and other tax revenues for subsidising a wide range of degrowth-compatible businesses and initiatives (see also Latouche 2009). As noted above, many such businesses and initiatives currently have few possibilities for gaining funding and encounter regulatory obstacles. As such, they would benefit from state involvement in the form of policies that in various ways support small-scale, local production, not-for-profit organisations and other alternative forms.

More controversially, to accomplish degrowth on a societal scale, the state may well have to nationalise dirty sectors, such as conventional monoculture, industries engaged in natural resource extraction and fossil fuels and companies producing chemicals, metals, mineral products and paper products.[3] The state would do so with a view to taking charge of either transforming ('greening') these sectors or dismantling them altogether (see Chapter 5). Such steps would have negative consequences relating to employment, and risk affecting the mental health of individuals employed in the sectors in question. Many of these individuals would be concerned about future occupation, pensions, meaning and identity. To alleviate these consequences, the state would need to proactively facilitate the reskilling of such employees and ensuring that genuinely green jobs are available.

Aside from reskilling for individuals leaving dirty industries, the degrowth state would provide free education for all and make available diverse options of education including higher education and vocational training. Moreover, the very nature of education would need to be transformed. Currently, the system of education is geared towards the reproduction of capitalist structures, whereas degrowth would require creating spaces for new imaginaries, reflection and critical approaches to capitalism and its structures, as well as emphasising genuine sustainability (Kaufmann et al. 2019). Educational pursuits of individuals can be facilitated by the state not only by making education accessible (free) and useful for a more sustainable future, but also by introducing supporting mechanisms which make education affordable and possible for everyone. Such mechanisms could include universal basic income, affordable housing and the provision of free services such as transportation, healthcare and childcare.

In terms of steering, the literature generally envisions degrowth transitions and societies to be profoundly democratic (Schmelzer et al. 2022). For instance, this may, in addition to representative democracy, involve more direct participatory decision-making, allowing citizens to be involved in taking decisions affecting their lives. This is relevant, for instance, in relation to green finance where, as we touched upon above, the state could play a key role. Its activities in this area could be guided or supported by various democratic forums. Relatedly, some scholars envision citizens' councils which facilitate public control over banking and financial regulation (e.g.,

Cahen-Fourot et al. 2022). Similar forums could be involved in deciding on tax-funded (low or no interest) green investments. Such a democratisation of green investments could be paralleled by steps taken by the state to reduce the space for investments by angel investors and venture capitalists. These forms of investment are widespread in capitalism (S. C. Parker 2018). They commonly entail the investors being entitled to a share in a business and its profit. Apart from putting immense pressure on the businesspersons to grow their businesses to repay debts, these forms of financing may alienate businesspersons from their business as a project and an idea since the investors acquire an opportunity to have a say in its matters. For more people to come to have a say on decisions in democratic forums, a redistribution (decentralisation) of power from the state to the local scale would be necessary (cf. Chapters 5 and 6).

As regards scale, degrowth scholarship has mainly focused on the local and the national levels (albeit see Fritz and Koch 2016; Koch 2015; Hasselbalch et al. 2023; Babic and Sharma 2023). Treatment of the international dimension has predominantly revolved around the Global North–Global South distinction, with many scholars arguing that degrowth mainly or exclusively concerns the Global North. While this is in some respects a fair argument, in others it is problematic: deep transformations across all four planes of social being are as relevant in the South as they are in the North, although the very different contexts are of course essential to take into consideration. Degrowth scholarship has yet to focus in any depth on the insertion of local and national scales into a global architecture. This is unfortunate, as it is difficult to imagine degrowth (national-scale) social formations functioning – or coming into being in the first place – in the absence of international coordination (see also Neilson 2020: 104).[4] Indeed, it is hard to envision one country succeeding in pursuing degrowth while all others remain integrated in the architecture of global capitalism. The state seems best positioned to ensure such coordination. That is, it makes more sense to coordinate international degrowth on the state level than the micro or grassroots level of individuals, businesses and movements. States can direct transformations in the international spaces and organisations they form part of (the EU, the OECD, the United Nations etc.).

The prevailing type of organisation of production and service provision in the growth-based economy is a large and growing business motivated by profit and owned by shareholders (Johanisova et al. 2013; Roman-Alcalá 2017). Such organisations are always in pursuit of minimising costs and maximising profit. They do so by externalising their costs to workers, the environment and future generations and exploiting nature, humans and non-humans. The competitive setting in which such organisations operate further facilitates this externalisation of costs and exploitation.

The whole world is viewed by such organisations as a resource pool and a market, while humans and nature are reduced to mere factors of production. Human desires for belonging, respect, comfort and so on are utilised by corporations as a platform for creation of wants. Many have pointed to multiple problems associated with such an inhuman scale of production and the inhumanity and alienation which derive from this scale, and called for human-scale production and production carried out in a humanistic way, with people and nature in mind (Schumacher 1993; Max-Neef 1991, 1992). For instance, for Max-Neef (1992), smallness or human scale indicates transparency, lack of bureaucracy and a relative ease of solving problems as they become manageable.

For Schumacher (1993), smallness meant lower ecological as well as social impact. Schumacher suggested that small-scale operations are less likely to be harmful to the environment than large-scale ones because their force is smaller in relation to the forces of nature. According to him, people organised in small units would take better care of natural resources than 'anonymous companies' which perceive the universe to be their quarry (Schumacher 1993: 23). The principles of production and business for a degrowth society have been known at least since the 1970s. Localisation, increased self-sufficiency, smallness and production to satisfy genuine human needs are some of those principles. However, more recently attempts have been made to more holistically outline what a business should look like in a degrowth society. While we discuss this in more detail in Chapter 6, here we briefly summarise the key aspects of degrowth business. First and foremost, business needs to be transformative of itself as well as the socio-economic structures of production. Transformations need to unfold in the domains of the business's material transactions with nature, people and non-humans and profit. In a degrowth society, production would be localised and place-sensitive, and, above all, humane.

It is important to recognise the nuance associated with business and degrowth transformations. For instance, not all businesses currently operating in the capitalist setting are large and profit-maximising, faceless and inhumane corporations. There are multiple examples of diverse forms of organising production (Gibson-Graham 2006). Not all businesses are striving to maximise their profits, exploit humans and nature and grow indefinitely. Cases in point are non-growing firms, lifestyle businesses and small-scale craft and artisanal production. Moreover, it is unrealistic to assume that degrowth transformation would, at least initially, entail conversion of all large-scale production into small-scale initiatives. Indeed, large-scale production is likely to remain in a degrowth society, while the principles – the reasons, ends, means and ownership patterns – under which such production is carried out would need to change substantially (see Chapter 6).

From capitalist diversity to degrowth diversity

A diversity of economies already exists alongside capitalism (Gibson-Graham 2006). Yet when moving from considering capitalism at an abstract level to considering its actual forms in specific spatio-temporal settings, it also becomes clear that capitalism itself continues to take a variety of forms – despite the pressures for convergence associated with economic globalisation and neoliberal policies. Aside from changing over time, institutional forms differ geographically. The field of comparative political economy is devoted to studying this diversity. Starting with the seminal work of Shonfield (1965), which identified a liberal model of capitalism typical of Britain, a statist model typical of France and a corporatist model typical of Germany, a range of typologies have been developed to aid the study of capitalist diversity. The most well-known examples are Esping-Andersen's three welfare regime ideal-types (Esping-Andersen 1990) and the 'varieties of capitalism' approach which distinguishes between coordinated and liberal market economies (Hall and Soskice 2001). Comparative political economy scholarship brings into focus how advanced capitalist countries differ with respect to their industrial relations systems, corporate governance arrangements, competition policy, the generosity of social transfers, and taxation and education systems, to give but a few examples.

Although the environment has generally been neglected by scholarship on capitalist diversity (Koch and Buch-Hansen 2021), such scholarship still provides important insight into the nature of capitalism, insights constituting a crucial supplement to the considerations of how institutional forms differed in Fordist versus neoliberal capitalism.[5] For example, Keynesian welfare states took a variety of forms, with the social democratic Scandinavian countries having welfare arrangements exhibiting a higher degree of decommodification than the conservative regime in Germany or the liberal one in the US (Esping-Andersen 1990). Fordism itself also varied among the advanced capitalist countries. For example, whereas Germany extensively introduced Fordist production techniques, in Denmark it was mainly the demand side of the Fordist growth model, that is, mass consumption of standardised goods, that manifested itself. In all its forms, however, Fordism relied on overexploitation of natural resources, not least in developing countries, where Fordism did not materialise. In a similar vein, a variety of competition states can be identified (Genschel and Seelkopf 2015).

When accounting for why different types of capitalism have emerged in different countries, one of the key factors pointed to by scholars of capitalist diversity are historical legacies of various kinds. For example, welfare regime scholarship has pointed to the importance of religious roots, noting that liberal welfare regimes mainly emerged in Protestant countries, whereas conservative welfare regimes typically appeared in countries dominated by Catholicism. Such scholarship also notes that the degree to which workers were organised in unions contributed to determining the nature of the welfare regime that emerged. In a similar vein, scholarship concerning the post-socialist countries in Central and Eastern Europe points out that institutional and cultural legacies mattered greatly in the transition from 'communism' to capitalism (Bohle and Greskovits 2007). Feldmann (2006), for example, identifies diverging legacies as a major reason why Estonia and Slovenia witnessed the emergence of fundamentally different varieties of capitalism.

The implications for degrowth transformations are vast. Aside from entailing systemic changes (Buch-Hansen and Carstensen 2021), such transformations would also entail incremental changes (Barlow et al. 2022) starting out from current social formations. That is, just as all capitalist societies took shape on the basis of what came before them, whether that was specific manifestations of feudalism or communism, so degrowth transformations, if they were in fact initiated on a wide scale, would to no small extent be shaped by the diverse structures, including institutional forms, of contemporary capitalism. Certainly, 'institutions can vary in their degree of path dependency, such that we can envisage institutions in the Anthropocene that are able to adapt to a rapidly changing (and potentially catastrophic) social-ecological context' (Dryzek 2016: 942). Still, path dependencies and ideational legacies would mean that instead of simply disappearing, existing forms would be recalibrated via a combination of existing practices and principles with new ones originating in various strands of thinking, including contemporary degrowth thinking. Within countries transformations would thus exhibit at least some continuity with the past, guaranteeing that a degrowth transformation in, say, Iceland would look very different from a degrowth transition in, say, Poland, Australia or Argentina (Buch-Hansen 2014; Buch-Hansen et al. 2016).

In conclusion

In this chapter the regulation theory concept of institutional forms was considered, first in relation to Fordist and neoliberal capitalism, then in relation to degrowth. Whereas institutional forms in capitalist social formations overall serve to facilitate capital accumulation (albeit not always successfully), we envision that under degrowth they would instead be oriented towards facilitating gentle social relations to nature and the satisfaction of basic human needs for all. Here we considered visions on the social relation to nature, the wage–labour nexus, the enterprise form, the nature of money, the state, and insertion into international regimes in relation to degrowth. Given that degrowth has yet to materialise on a societal level, and given that it would vary from one setting to the next, no attempt was made to outline more than the contours of how the institutional forms could look in degrowth social formations. Nor was an attempt made to specify their hierarchy, although it was suggested that, in comparison to under neoliberal capitalism, (gentle) social relations to nature would be placed high in the hierarchy, whereas the monetary regime would take a less prominent position.

The idea would be for the various institutional forms to entangle and produce synergies. For example, the state and international organisations may oversee green finance, channelling economic resources to degrowth-compatible businesses, creating meaningful green employment. Participation in/working for degrowth-compatible businesses, which opens spaces for deviation from profit maximisation and shorter working hours, would allow individuals to dedicate more time towards taking part in direct democracy, thus having an impact on how the state makes decisions and shapes society's relations to nature. A similar effect of increased participation in direct democracy can be achieved, for instance, by the state providing universal basic income. Demonetisation of spaces, such as producing one's own food and energy, may require more time spent in and with nature and working with the land and nature more closely, thus deeply transforming and reshaping social (and individual) relations to nature. In turn, a transformed relation to nature may encourage people to participate differently in other spaces such as business and democracy and seek meaningful employment and education for genuine sustainability.

Notes

1 One strand of critical political economy research speaks, for example, of social structures of accumulation to denote the set of institutions that serve to stabilise the capital accumulation process in specific times and places (e.g., McDonough et al. 2010).

2 In this context it can be noted that in the degrowth literature proposals for both minimum and maximum incomes are discussed (e.g., Buch-Hansen and Koch 2019; Hickel 2020).

3 On the delay tactics currently used by the petrochemical industry to avoid genuine sustainability transitions, see Tilsted et al. (2022).

4 On how to combine such coordination with localised, human-scale development, cf. Max-Neef (1991).

5 Because mainstream (constructivist and rationalist) comparative political economy scholarship studies capitalism as if nature does not matter, critical issues become none-issues in such research. This is seen in how economic growth is viewed, namely in an altogether one-sided (positive) manner. GDP growth is regarded as the most important measure of economic performance and is thus widely used as the key parameter for comparing how successful specific countries are. With inspiration from mainstream economics, 'good' institutions are seen as those capable of delivering high GDP and productivity growth rates, while 'bad' institutions are those delivering the opposite (Amable and Palombarini 2009: 123–124). The massive ecological downsides of capitalist growth are neglected (Koch and Buch-Hansen 2021; see also Loewen 2022). Although all forms of capitalism inflict harm on nature, there are still differences in their social relations to nature (Cahen-Fourot 2020). Differences also pertain to access to nature, ranging from restricted access rights in the UK to Everyman's rights in some Scandinavian countries.

3

Theorising deep transformations

Capitalism, with its growth imperative, is a key structure – or rather web of social structures – that degrowth as an anti- *and* post-capitalist political project aspires to transform. To initiate the theorisation of how this deep transformation can be accomplished, the present chapter draws on insights from contemporary political economy scholarship, mainly but not solely research and theoretical perspectives in the historical materialist tradition. A range of historical materialist perspectives – including regulation theory (Boyer 1990; Koch 2012; Staricco 2017), the social structures of accumulation approach (Gordon et al. 1982; McDonough et al. 2010) and transnational historical materialism (Cox 1987; Overbeek 2013) – all seek to explain when and why institutional and societal changes take place. In what follows, we distil various prerequisites for deep transformative change from such scholarship (see also Buch-Hansen 2018; Koch 2015), supplementing it with insights from, for example, anarchism and scholarship on diverse economies. We draw on such additional literatures because degrowth as conceptualised in the Introduction would entail transformations the depths of which necessitate a theorisation going well beyond what critical political economy (or any other single field) can provide. This is the case because degrowth entails metamorphoses not only of social structures and relationships, but also of the inner being of individuals and the social relation to nature. Moreover, the range of actors, structures and processes such perspectives ascribe importance to may not suffice to theorise degrowth transformations in a holistic manner.

The political economy of capitalist transformations

As noted in Chapter 2, the institutional forms making up a mode of regulation stabilise capitalism. They 'codify the fundamental social relations that shape a given kind of capitalism. … They stabilize and normalize social conflicts and power struggles amongst antagonistic social groups or classes. They embody political compromises between them and ensure the reproducibility of the system until the next major crisis' (Cahen-Fourot 2020: 3). Far from emerging automatically in response to the 'needs' of an accumulation regime, then, a mode of regulation is the outcome of political conflicts and struggles. When focusing on such conflicts and struggles, critical political economists ascribe much importance to the social forces engendered by the capitalist production process, namely fractions of capital and labour. These social forces are regarded as the most important drivers of social change. The 'members' of a class fraction perform similar economic functions in the process of capital accumulation and, consequently, tend to have specific ideological inclinations (van der Pijl 1998). Seen from a class fraction perspective, Fordist capitalism was underpinned by a 'historic bloc' comprising a coalition between the dominant fraction of industrial capital and bank capital and organised labour (van Apeldoorn 2002: 52).

The outcomes of struggles between class fractions to no small extent depend on the relative power they command. It is, for instance, far from coincidental that wage and wealth inequalities in the advanced capitalist countries were much lower in the 1960s than now: trade unions in Fordism – in the context of full employment of the (male) workforce and much smaller geographical capital mobility – were in a much better bargaining position than is the case in today's globalised, finance-driven and flexible accumulation regime (Koch 2012; Leonardi 2019). This also goes to show that over time, social forces undergo transformations through dialectical interplays with the capitalist system itself, and in this process, power relations change and socio-economic transformations become possible (Wigger and Buch-Hansen 2014).

This brings us to the topic of structural crises. Seen from the vantage point of critical political economy, capitalism is a crisis-prone economic system. This insight has roots in the works of Marx, the scholar to discover that capitalism is replete with contradictions causing harm to people, other species and the planet (Collier 2004). Institutional forms can temporarily provide a fix to many of these contradictions, but eventually all modes of regulation break down because they can no longer sustain capital accumulation. Structural crises are crises necessitating the appearance of a new accumulation regime and mode of regulation to allow for continued capital accumulation (Boyer and Saillard 2002). Upsetting existing arrangements and throwing 'social and class forces into states of flux and reorganization that involve struggles over hegemony' (Robinson 2014: 217), such crises constitute moments when deep change can happen. Ultimately, structural crises can pave the way for new historic blocs, accumulation regimes, institutional forms and modes of regulation. An example of a structural crisis leading to such changes was the crisis of Fordist capitalism in the 1970s. The crisis, which had multiple causes (see e.g., van Apeldoorn 2002; Jessop

2002; Kotz and McDonough 2010), was impossible to resolve within the framework of existing institutional forms, some of which started (or were perceived) to undermine the capital accumulation process. The extensive Keynesian welfare states were cases in point. Eventually a new neoliberal form of capitalism materialised in the Western world and elsewhere. Neoliberal ideas came to prevail because they were developed into a political project that a powerful constellation of actors came to perceive as in their interest and thus advocated (Stahl 2019).

Three phases can be delineated in the process of a political project becoming hegemonic, namely phases of deconstruction, construction and consolidation (van Apeldoorn and Overbeek 2012). In its *deconstructive phase*, neoliberal ideas provided intellectual ammunition for the disruption of the post-Second World War social order of embedded liberalism/social democracy. Neoclassical economists and right-wing (organic) intellectuals such as Friedrich von Hayek and Milton Friedman played an important role in questioning existing institutional arrangements such as the Keynesian welfare state and in devising the emerging neoliberal project (Peck 2010). Characterised by 'a mix of liberal pro-market and supply-side discourses (laissez-faire, privatization, liberalization, deregulation, competitiveness) and of monetarist orthodoxy (price stability, balanced budgets, austerity)' (van Apeldoorn and Overbeek 2012: 5), the neoliberal project provided a clear alternative to the Fordist type of capitalism and came to be widely perceived as providing convincing solutions to its crisis.

In the *constructive phase*, neoliberal ideas increasingly achieved the status of being the only game in town. Countless policies and reforms came to be shaped by such ideas. Corporate actors played a major role in these developments. For example, research has documented how, against the backdrop of economic crises, German and Swedish employers created and funded think tanks and public relations campaigns that led to neoliberal reforms of existing institutions (Kinderman 2017). The research finds that 'these think-tanks have facilitated processes … that have led to a marked transformation of the German and Swedish social models and of German and Swedish capitalism over the past decades' (2017: 590). In the final, *consolidative phase*, neoliberal policies had been widely implemented, albeit with major variations from one country to the next (Brenner et al. 2010). At this point, the neoliberal project had become hegemonic in most parts of the capitalist world in that the ideas underpinning it had become 'common sense', something to which also subordinate groups lent their consent (Robinson 2014).

Neoliberal capitalism primarily served (and serves) the interest of the fraction of transnational financial capital (Overbeek and van der Pijl 1993). This fraction came to lead a historic bloc which also comprised other leading transnational corporations, the middle classes and even organised labour (van Apeldoorn and Overbeek 2012: 5). The latter was, however, in a much weaker position than had been the case under Fordist capitalism, due, for instance, to overseas competition, declining union membership, weaker links to social-democratic parties and changes in the nature of work. From the late 1970s onwards, the balance of class power gradually shifted (Baccaro and Howell 2017: 176–177).

What are the implications of the above reflections of capitalist transformations for degrowth? That is, what of value to degrowth transformations can we learn from critical political economy scholarship on past transformations? As argued elsewhere (Buch-Hansen 2018), at least four prerequisites for deep socio-economic change can be derived from such scholarship: a deep crisis, an alternative political project, a comprehensive coalition of social forces, and public consent. When considering these prerequisites, it is important to be mindful that degrowth on a societal scale would involve *systemic* transformations, that is, transformations that are far more comprehensive and profound than those seen in the context of shifts from one type of capitalism to another (Buch-Hansen and Carstensen 2021).

Deep crisis

The first prerequisite for socio-economic transformations is deep crisis. As noted in the previous section, critical political economists use the notion of a structural crisis to denote crises that cannot be resolved within the existing type of capitalism. For capital accumulation to resume in the face of such a crisis, a new accumulation regime with a new mode of regulation is required. Structural crises, then, give rise to transformations within the framework of capitalism. Yet if degrowth entails systemic change, then a prerequisite for it to materialise may be a *systemic crisis*. A systemic crisis is one that can only be resolved if the economic system itself is changed. As such, it 'involves the replacement of a system by an entirely new system *or* leads to an outright collapse' (Robinson 2014: 129). Such a crisis may also be thought of in terms of a 'crisis in the dominant mode of production', implying that 'no new accumulation regime can emerge, even taking into account the ability of institutional forms to adapt' (Boyer and Saillard 2002: 43–44).

As noted in the Introduction to the present book, humanity currently faces not one but several deep and intertwined crises, including a social crisis, a political crisis and the escalating biodiversity and climate crises. These crises would seem to constitute something approaching a systemic crisis in that it is difficult to see how capitalism can survive them. It says quite a lot when one of the leading social scientists of our time asks not whether but *how* capitalism will end (Streeck 2016). In Streeck's analysis, capitalism is in its final crisis, partly because it is collapsing from its own contradictions, partly because it has defeated its traditionally most powerful opponents. That is, whereas in the past capitalism's enemies (say, the labour movement) often forced it to assume a new form, thereby rescuing it from itself, today its enemies are too weak to push through such changes (2016: 13).

In the Introduction we noted that the climate and biodiversity crises will eventually undermine capitalism itself. Yet unfortunately capitalism will, in all likelihood, not end until long after it has made the earth uninhabitable for most human and non-human beings. As Malm (2018: 194) puts it, 'there is little evidence that profitability is under any atmospheric sword of Damocles, but plenty of proof that people with no advanced means of production occupy such a position'. Consequently, he warns against eagerly anticipating 'the imminent climate-induced collapse of the capitalist mode of production' (2018: 195). Harvey (2014: 254–255) makes the related observation that capitalism thrives on localised catastrophes caused by climatic changes. Such catastrophes not only constitute business opportunities, they also serve to mask that it is capitalism itself, rather than the unruliness and unpredictability of 'mother nature', that is their root cause. If the climate and biodiversity crises will not in themselves bring about the end of capitalism, the ensemble of crises they form part of may nonetheless contribute to facilitating such an outcome. Indeed, if deep crisis is a precondition for deep change, today's world is certainly a world in which such change ought to be possible.

The articulation of a political project

The second prerequisite for the degrowth vision to materialise is that it informs an alternative political project, based on which policymakers and other agents can interpret reality and act. In the opening paragraph of this chapter, we referred to degrowth as a political project. Yet whether degrowth constitutes a political project of course depends on what is understood by such a project. If we take it to mean a full-fledged political programme with detailed policies with which all those embracing the concept agree, then degrowth is not a political project. As mentioned in the introductory chapter, proponents of degrowth neither agree on one definition of the concept, nor on what it would take for degrowth to materialise on various scales (the local, national and transnational) in different locations. For example, as we come back to in Chapter 5, some degrowth advocates are critical of the state owing to their own political/philosophical convictions, shaped for example by anarchist perspectives (such as anarcho-primitivism). Others may be anti- or non-state oriented because they have experienced too many statist barriers to transformations (Liegey and Nelson 2020: 137–138).

Still, most advocates of degrowth seem to take the position that democratically adopted top-down policies are an important precondition for degrowth transformations to materialise.[1] In the literature on degrowth, a wide variety of policies are being proposed and discussed (Fitzpatrick et al. 2022). To mention but a few, these relate to, for example, promoting work-sharing and reduced working time (Schor 2015), placing a ceiling on income and wealth (Buch-Hansen and Koch 2019), taxing high-carbon luxury goods (Gough 2017), placing limits on flights and reducing the number of planes and airports (Hassler et al. 2019), providing sustainable welfare benefits, for instance in the form of universal basic vouchers (Bohnenberger 2020), banning advertising (Latouche 2009) and introducing regulation compelling companies to introduce extended warranties on products to remove their incentive to design products with a short lifespan, as well as regulation making it illegal for companies to produce products that cannot be repaired (Hickel 2020: 211). Many of the discussed policies are *eco-social* policies, that is, policies that simultaneously advance the goals of environmental sustainability and social equity (Gough 2017). For example, train tickets and other forms of slow travel are unaffordable to many, just as organic foods are considerably more expensive than inorganic food. As a result, many people fly and eat inorganic food. Subsidising train tickets and organic food would serve the purpose of making more sustainable diets and forms of transportation affordable to all.

In later chapters we return to some of these policies, exploring them in greater depth. In the present context it suffices to note that if we understand a political project to denote a general vision of a different society that points beyond the major crises of our time, a vision that is accompanied by discussion of policies and initiatives that can materialise it, then degrowth does qualify as a political project (see also Alexander and Gleeson 2022: 59). Degrowth is, however, a political project in a different sense from how this notion is often used in critical political economy scholarship, in that this literature for the most part focuses on political projects aiming to transform but not move beyond capitalism. Van Apeldoorn and Overbeek (2012: 5) write that 'any hegemonic project needs … a more or less coherent accumulation strategy serving the interests of the leading capital fraction and their immediate allies'. Degrowth is neither premised on benefiting any capital fraction nor is it a political project that comes with an accumulation strategy. If anything, it offers a vision of 'de-accumulation' in many sectors of the economy and it aspires to benefit not merely humans but also nature and non-human beings – now and in the future.

Mobilising a comprehensive coalition of social forces

For a political project to shape societal developments, a comprehensive coalition of social forces with sufficient power and resources needs to find it attractive and worth fighting for. As noted above, critical political economy scholarship gives primacy to the social forces rooted in the capitalist production process, that is, representatives of different fractions of capital and labour. The power balance between these social forces is regarded as a key determinant of overall societal developments. Degrowth is, however, different from traditional political projects in that it is not class-based. Inevitably, those advocating degrowth are rooted in classes, most of them probably in the middle classes, yet degrowth is not a project aspiring to promote the interests of this or other classes – or only human beings. Liegey and Nelson observe that 'being a degrowth activist sets one apart from traditional class identities as the movement fights for a class-free world' (2020: 128). Currently, the main proponents of degrowth are grassroots, small fractions of left-wing parties and labour unions, as well as academics and other citizens who are concerned about the looming eco-social collapse. In other words, those who promote degrowth do it not because they themselves stand to gain more from its realisation than would others, but because they believe that it is necessary if the current and future needs of human beings and other species are to be met (see Chapter 7).

Seen from a critical political economy perspective, the problem is that the social forces currently supporting degrowth are far from powerful enough for this project to come to shape wider socio-economic developments. Leading political parties, labour unions, business associations and international organisations have yet to embrace degrowth – indeed, they typically strongly support economic growth, perceiving no desirable alternative to it. That none of the powerful actors in advanced capitalist societies finds it appealing has been identified as 'the weakest spot in the degrowth project' (Barca et al. 2019: 6). The resources of the degrowth movement are modest, certainly compared to the resources commanded by those who were successful in promoting projects that became hegemonic in the past. For example, it is in a far weaker position than was the labour union movement under Fordist capitalism, and its resources are dwarfed by those available to those representing corporate interests in contemporary neoliberal capitalism. It is not just the degrowth project that finds itself in this situation; more generally, no alternative project to the currently still prevailing neoliberal project, let alone to capitalism as an economic system, enjoys support from a coalition of social forces strong enough to make deep social change a reality. Indeed, this is the main reason why neoliberalism and capitalism linger on.

Streeck (2016: 36) puts it this way: 'Before capitalism will go to hell … it will for the foreseeable future hang in limbo, dead or about to die from an overdose of itself but still very much around, as nobody will have the power to move its decaying body out of the way.'

In Barca's analysis, attracting support from 'ecologically minded' members of the global middle classes who are willing to consume and work less does not suffice if the degrowth project is to shape overall societal developments. In her words, the project will 'remain politically weak unless it manages to enter into dialogue with a broadly defined global working class – including both wage labor and the myriad forms of work that support it – and its organizations' (2019: 214). This is undoubtedly true. Yet to imagine a coalition powerful enough to bring about degrowth, it is necessary to transcend the class-based perspectives of historical materialist critical political economy. No single type of actor is powerful enough to make it happen. Degrowth transformations can only materialise through the combined actions of myriad actors positioned in states, civil society and business. Related to this, diverse economies scholars Gibson-Graham and Dombroski (2020) place hope in the movements and activism that young people, women and Indigenous peoples engage in globally. They note, for instance, that 'because women are everywhere and therefore always somewhere, change can be enacted in all those many somewheres' (2020: 20). Important insights can also be gleaned from anarchist thinking, according to which the successor project of capitalism is already in the process of being built within micro-level bottom-up initiatives that exist at the margins of contemporary neoliberal capitalism, such as cooperatives and sustainable communities (Chomsky 1999: 138; Wigger and Buch-Hansen 2013; see also Bärnthaler 2023). Given the depth of change that degrowth transformations entail, and the speed with which they would need to happen, it is, however, just as improbable that they could materialise solely through bottom-up, grassroots initiatives as it is improbable that they can emerge solely via top-down policies. And just as degrowth cannot be realised without policies implemented by state apparatuses at the local, national and transnational scales, so it cannot come about without the involvement of businesses and large groups of citizens.

In terms of temporality, the various policies that are being discussed in degrowth circles are unlikely to *initiate* degrowth transformations; rather, such policies are more likely to be the *outcome* of the efforts of social movements and other actors in civil society (Alexander and Gleeson 2022). In the current ideological environment, it would be political suicide for most political parties to embrace the aforementioned policies. For degrowth transformations to be initiated, a massive civil society mobilisation, combined with a surge in degrowth-compatible business (Nesterova 2020a, 2020b,

2021a) would be required. If such a mobilisation of growth-critical and socio-ecological social forces were to gain a decisive momentum, it could make it attractive, or at least feasible, for political parties and states to pursue degrowth policies (Koch 2022a). The outcome could be 'a combination of bottom-up mobilisations and action and top-down regulation, resulting in a new mix of property forms including communal, state, and individual property and a new division of labour between market, state, and "commons"' (Koch 2020b: 127). The thousands of degrowth-compatible micro-level civil society and business initiatives that are mushrooming in recent years may, together with various social movements (Burkhart et al. 2020), come to provide the basis for a mobilisation of a comprehensive coalition of social forces.

Building consent

The final prerequisite for degrowth to happen on a wider scale is popular consent to its overall vision. There are some indications that growth-critical ideas are gaining ground. A petition run by the European Environmental Bureau, which inter alia called on the European Union, its institutions and member states to devise policies for post-growth futures and reconsider the pursuit of growth as an overarching policy goal, was signed by more than 90,000 people. Drews et al. (2019: 150) suggest, based on data on Spain, that 'a considerable part of the population exhibits sceptical views about growth'. Even so, it is safe to say that overall there is no consent to the idea of degrowth in the advanced capitalist countries. In fact, the vast majority of people in these countries are unlikely to have heard of degrowth. If this observation is correct, it speaks volumes of just how marginalised the idea of degrowth remains, even if it has gained traction over the past decade. But it is not just that many people are unaware of the idea of degrowth, it is also that it is doubtful that they, if they were to hear about it, would consider it a good idea to move beyond capitalism to a system with reduced and different production and consumption. One reason why degrowth may not be intuitively appealing to many people in the advanced capitalist countries and beyond is that it is incompatible with the Western norm of consumption (Brand and Wissen 2013; Koch 2012) and more generally the Western view of nature.[2] If degrowth were to materialise, most citizens in the rich countries would have to adapt to a materially lower standard of living. Limits placed – in one way or another – on car ownership, flights, accommodation forms, diets and other environmentally damaging aspects of the Western norm of consumption would go against currently prevailing understandings of what constitutes a good life. As such they would, to put it mildly, not be popular. A further reason why consent to degrowth would be difficult to achieve is that advocates of the green growth discourse and other pro-market ideologies have been successful in creating the illusion that companies, markets and new technologies will take care of the problems so that people will not have to change their lifestyles in major ways.

Nevertheless, there are cracks in the hegemony of the pro-growth discourse. In Germany, a country with strong environmental movements that have, for instance, advanced sufficiency and reduction of working hours, labour unions have traditionally sided with business and the state in fighting for 'a good life of consumption' and 'the right to work' (Komlosy 2018). Yet recent research finds that previously hegemonic views are called into question within major German unions, with counter-hegemonic views as to what a good life entails being expressed to varying degrees (Keil and Kreinin 2022). Although this obviously does not mean that these unions now consent to degrowth – far from it – it does suggest that there are openings for consent to other views on work, production and growth than the currently prevailing view.

The word consent derives from Latin where it means 'feel together'. Further to this, consent to degrowth is not something that could be imposed on individuals or something that can be reduced to a question of social structures and social interactions. Consent would require individuals to feel that degrowth is a sensible development and welcome degrowth practices in their everyday life and in society at large. For this to happen, self-transformation at the level of individuals is required. Such self-transformation could, for instance, involve taking steps from the 'mode of having' to the 'mode of being' (Fromm 2013). As noted in Chapter 1, the mode of having entails an outlook revolving around possessions, accumulation and status. By contrast, the mode of being revolves around focusing on who we are as humans and our capacities for learning, loving, caring, altruism, solidarity, forgiveness, presence, joyfulness and so on. We deal in greater length with this matter in Chapter 4. In the present context it suffices to observe that without such self-transformations it is difficult to imagine that degrowth – with its logic evolving around gentleness and care for humans, non-human species and nature more generally – could materialise and work. There is no single source of transformations of this kind. Rather, various combinations of a multitude of causal mechanisms could bring them about. These mechanisms could include interactions with people and with social structures and experiences in and with nature, and involve becoming aware of new and gentler ways of relating to the world (see also Conclusion, this volume).

In conclusion

> Capitalism will never fall on its own. It will have to be pushed. The accumula-
> tion of capital will never cease. It will have to be stopped. The capitalist class
> will never willingly surrender its power. It will have to be dispossessed.
>
> (Harvey 2010: 260)

Harvey notes that the task of stopping capital accumulation and dispos-
sessing the capitalist class requires a strong social movement with a strong
political vision of an alternative around which a collective political subjectivity can revolve (Harvey 2014). In this chapter, we have pointed to some
of the same prerequisites for degrowth to materialise on a societal scale, yet
pointing also to the importance of consent, self-transformation and crisis.
Although the current economic system finds itself in a deep structural or
even systemic crisis, a key prerequisite for deep social change, it is of course
by no means a given conclusion that such change will take the form of
degrowth. While the current crises facing advanced capitalist democracies
can be seen to have paved the way for progressive social forces, they have
also facilitated the rise of right-wing populism and authoritarianism.

Moreover, as noted in the Introduction, powerful actors (corporations,
governments, international organisations and unions) have so far primarily
responded to the climate and biodiversity crises by embracing the political project of 'green growth' – at least at the level of discourse. Beyond its
green rhetoric, the corporate world does not stand united behind this project. Ougaard (2016), for instance, speaks of a conflict line between transnational companies involved in the extraction and processing of coal, oil
and gas, thus having a material interest in the carbon-based economy, and
companies that have a material interest in decarbonisation. Examples of
the latter include 'producers of equipment for renewable energy production
and companies that stand to lose from the consequences of global warming,
such as insurance companies' (Ougaard 2016: 467; see also Buch-Hansen
and Carstensen 2021). Within business, then, there is no universal consent
to the green growth project. Going forward, the main challenge for this project is the anomaly at its heart, that is, the lack of evidence to suggest that
it is possible to rapidly and drastically bring down CO_2 emissions while the
economy keeps growing exponentially. As the gap between, on one hand,
the green growth discourse and, on the other, the material reality of increasing CO_2 emissions, climate emergency and biodiversity loss widens in the
years to come, it may become increasingly difficult to uphold the illusion
that the green growth project delivers a serious response to the predicament
humanity is in. Against this background, degrowth ideas may come to enjoy
wider consent.

Notes

1 Or, in the case of anarchists who find it better to side with Marxist than pro-capitalist views, top-down policies and government involvement are seen as a necessary evil.
2 Whereas in the Western view nature is seen as composed of objects, under degrowth, nature would be seen as composed of subjects (cf. Rodman, 1983).

4

Civil society in degrowth transformations

Civil society is where ideas challenging the growth paradigm could come to prevail and where a shift away from the current consumer culture could happen. Civil society is a space in which more citizens could come to experiment with alternative, sustainable forms of living. Civil society is the site of degrowth activism, the site in which the degrowth movement can form alliances with other movements (Burkhart et al. 2020). And civil society is the realm in which broad consent to, and a demand for, profound eco-social transformations could arise, prompting policymakers to adopt more ambitious policies. Certainly actors in other sites are also of key importance if degrowth is to happen on a societal scale, states (Chapter 5) and businesses (Chapter 6) being cases in point. Yet on their own they cannot bring degrowth about. In short, then, changes in – and emanating from – civil society are an essential part of degrowth transformations. Enriching the theoretical perspective outlined in the previous chapters, in this chapter we conceptualise civil society and we reflect on its scales and diversity in degrowth transformations. Moreover, we highlight the importance of individual self-transformation for civil society to become a sufficiently potent driving force towards degrowth.

Conceptualising civil society

Civil society is a broad social domain rather than a 'thing'. It can be defined *negatively* by what it is not: it excludes the state and business, though it is inherently interconnected with them.[1] For example, members of civil society interact with businesses as businesspersons, employees, customers, activists, organisations and so on. The same person can run a business (and thus belong to the site of 'business') and be a member of, say, a degrowth network or volunteer for a charity (and thus belong to the site of the 'civil society'). Some forms of business or organisations involved in production of goods and services belong to the sites of both civil society and business.

This applies, for instance, to consumer-producer arrangements such as community-supported agriculture, politically inclined cooperatives and eco-social enterprises. Still, civil society as a site excludes business.

Civil society can also be defined *positively* by what it encompasses: a plenitude of relationships and commitments between humans and various social structures and entities (civil society organisations) outside the state and business. This implies that civil society refers to many very diverse formal and informal 'social forms', such as community organisations, networks, trade unions, voluntary associations, non-government organisations and academia. Often, then, civil society is 'understood to refer to the realm of autonomous group action distinct from both corporate power and the state' (Cox 1999: 19). Yet the associations, encounters, organisations, networks etc. of civil society rest on the voluntary actions of individuals (Adloff 2021: 151). As such it is important not to separate social forms in civil society from what makes them possible, namely individuals. Thus, we include human individuals in our contemplation of civil society transformations.

The concept of civil society has a long history. Cox (1999: 7–8) identifies two broad understandings of civil society in capitalist settings. The first is a top-down understanding in which civil society is regarded as a site in which the prevailing social forces form a hegemony, so as to secure the population's consent to the social order. The other is a bottom-up understanding which views civil society as a site from which groups and classes can build a counter-hegemony that can challenge and ultimately replace the previous hegemonic order.

Further to this, in relation to degrowth transformations we propose viewing civil society as a site as well a force of transformations. On one hand, civil society is a *site of transformations* due to its existing and potential role of being the space where diverse and multiple emancipatory transformations occur and where new ones begin. Civil society is 'the realm of contesting ideas in which the intersubjective meanings upon which people's sense of "reality" are based can become transformed and new concepts of the natural order of society can emerge' (Cox 1999: 10). Transformations do not, of course, necessarily point in the direction of degrowth, and it should also be kept in mind that the activities of individuals and groups can contribute to reproducing existing ideas and social forms in civil society rather than transform them. The hegemony of particular ideologies, path dependencies and material interests are some of the mechanisms facilitating this outcome. Also, it should not be assumed that actors in civil society are civilised, democratically minded or tolerant. Forces in civil society can be uncivil, reactionary, violent etc., and more generally civil society is better understood as a plural, unequal and sometimes conflicting site than as an equal and harmonious public sphere (Gready and Robins 2017).

It is thus important not to romanticise civil society, seeing it as the domain of hope for degrowth while regarding, for example, the state and business as an enemy thereof. Instead, the ways in which existing civil society forms can and do contribute to the status quo and even deterioration rather than to emancipation and degrowth transformations should be recognised. For instance, academia to a large extent reproduces capitalist structures (M. Parker 2018). In a degrowth society it would undergo a significant transformation and would need to adopt a different approach to what it means and entails to educate and take part in people's growth as human beings and citizens. Likewise, some networks and movements within civil society can organise for and pursue political agendas and worldviews which are incompatible with degrowth, right-wing ideologies being an example. Having said that, in civil society one can also find many examples of empowering, counter-hegemonic social forms (Gibson-Graham 2006; see also Ehrnström-Fuentes and Biese 2022). They include, for instance, various alternative social groups, intentional communities and alternative organisations of production.

Civil society is a *force of transformation* because humans not only reproduce, but also intentionally transform social structures (Bhaskar 1989; Buch-Hansen and Nielsen 2020; Hartwig 2007). Participation in civil society organisations can entail a step away from the assumption that transformations can be brought about merely individually (for example, by changing one's consumption patterns) and exploring and strengthening various existing non-capitalist and anti-capitalist civil forms together with one's fellow humans. Despite its relative separation from the state, civil society is *political*. That is, with their activities, civil society organisations, as well as individuals within civil society, support and manifest particular worldviews, ideologies, affiliations and visions of the future. Different social forms in civil society are forces aiming for different kinds and degrees of transformation. For example, trade unions for the most part operate within a pro-capitalist, pro-growth horizon and do not seek deep societal transformations. At the other end of the spectrum, the degrowth movement is an example of a force in civil society which repoliticises topics such as the primacy of economic growth while aiming for a post-capitalist social order.

The political nature of civil society can also be manifested in implicit political and ethical commitments such as in everyday and largely degrowth-compatible activism without an explicit reference to degrowth. For instance, the voluntary simplicity movement (Elgin 2013) is largely degrowth compatible but not explicitly degrowth oriented. Whether explicitly oriented towards degrowth or not, important principles for civil society to play a role in degrowth transformations are cooperation and organisation of, and in, alternative-to-capitalism arrangements and social forms (Trainer 2012) and realising their benefits for transforming the current society towards one co-existing harmoniously with nature and within itself. These alternatives may include networks which advocate degrowth, community organisations, trade unions and others. Importantly, such initiatives and forms do not have to be created from nothing. Degrowth-compatible alternatives already exist in society alongside capitalist structures (Gibson-Graham 2006), contributing to prefiguring a degrowth society.

A prerequisite for civil society coming to act as a stronger force of degrowth transformations may be that individuals in civil society seek out, learn about and participate more in such alternatives. Having said that, it remains essential not to assume that collective actions, though important and necessary, are suitable for everyone. Thus, some members of civil society may prefer to participate in degrowth transformations without actively participating in organisations by, for example, pursuing a different way of living focused on solitude or co-presence with non-humans and nature. Suggesting organising as *the* solution and organisation as *the* mode of participation in degrowth transformations may be alienating, and this is something degrowth cannot afford, considering the limited support the movement currently enjoys (Chapter 3).

Civil society never exists in a vacuum. Its nature, and the nature of the role different social forms in civil society can play in degrowth transformations, varies from one setting to the next. For instance, in countries characterised by the liberal form of capitalism, transformations would likely arise from social movements, while in countries with coordinated forms of capitalism, that is, where trade unions are strong and welfare provision ensured, 'a process of "negotiated de-growth" – involving a societal compromise between governments and employers' and employees' organisations as well as various interest and expert groups – may be envisaged' (Buch-Hansen 2014: 170). Finally, in countries where capitalism is state led, degrowth transformations are more likely to originate from the state while also being influenced by social movements and organisational practices (Buch-Hansen 2014).

Scales and diversity of civil society in degrowth transformations

Civil society varies across different scales as well as across different fields. Fields can be seen as relatively autonomous societal arenas characterised by particular activities, strategies, forms of capital and rules (Bourdieu 2014). What can be done by an individual on their own is different to what can be achieved by a larger social organisation. The change that can be implemented in, say, academia is different to change that can be manifested in, say, community organisations. Having said that, there are overlaps, common underlying principles as well as possibilities for different forms of civil society to work together. Seen from the vantage point of the theoretical perspective unfolded in the present book, then, no particular social form or scale of civil society should be given primacy in relation to degrowth transformations. Rather, a prerequisite for such transformations to occur are civil society activities spanning multiple scales and social forms.

Starting at the micro level, this is where initiatives appear to be potentially most in line with the eco-anarchist strand of thought within degrowth (e.g., Trainer 2012, 2014). Eco-anarchism advocates a highly localised and self-governing mode of social living. This strand of thought places hope in various small-scale community organisations and requires multiple civil society organisations. That is, the social life that eco-anarchism envisions must be practised collectively. Community gardens and orchards, reclaiming of previously industrial spaces, local currencies and repair workshops cannot be implemented by isolated individuals. Thus, as highlighted by eco-anarchists within degrowth, a high level of cooperation is required alongside participation and democratic decision-making (Trainer 2012). The eco-anarchist way of life, in other words, relies fully on civil society and not on the state or business. The only desired type of businesses are very small-scale, privately owned companies (Trainer 2012), most likely craft or artisanal producers.

While local initiatives such as community gardens and local currencies are by definition localised, movements do not have to be constrained to a certain town, urban space (Schmid 2022) or region. They can span the globe. As mentioned above, some movements are explicitly degrowth orientated while others are implicitly degrowth compatible. Degrowth itself is a broad movement within civil society (Buch-Hansen 2021), a movement embodying a plurality of, in some cases, conflicting views. For instance, the political alignment of the degrowth movement remains unclear if not contradictory: while some advocate for eco-socialism, others advocate eco-anarchism. This diversity has led to the suggestion that it makes sense to speak about degrowths in the plural rather than of a single degrowth movement (Nesterova 2022b).

Apart from the degrowth movement itself, there are multiple existing civil society movements which can be degrowth compatible (Burkhart et al. 2020). The Transition movement is a case in point. In the words of its co-founder Rob Hopkins, it constitutes 'a social experiment on a massive scale' (2011: 16). It was established in 2006 in the English town Totnes, and subsequently spread rapidly to several parts of the world. The core purpose of the Transition movement is to address climate change and peak oil by building community resilience. With a view to reducing carbon emissions and oil dependence significantly, those involved in Transition initiatives seek to make their communities self-reliant with respect to energy and food production, waste and transport. Like ecovillages, Transition initiatives differ substantially, owing to varying local conditions and because they build on community experience and knowledge instead of relying on external experts or one-size-fits-all recipes. For instance, there are Transition initiatives in villages, towns, cities, universities, neighbourhoods and districts. Everywhere they are rooted in local cultures. Consequently, 'Transition in Brazil, emerging with a distinctly Brazilian flavour, will look very different from Transition in Edinburgh or in New Zealand' (Hopkins 2011: 74).

Other movements which are generally degrowth compatible are, for instance, voluntary simplicity, zero-waste and minimalism. These movements are not without challenges both in terms of their practice and definition. For instance, minimalism can be viewed as a movement driven by aesthetics rather than by ethics, specific political or philosophical commitments, or respect towards nature. It does not require a non-anthropocentric philosophical perspective to be practised (on minimalism, see Nesterova 2023). The aspirational zero-waste movement likewise focuses on the level of personal consumption, though some adherents may participate in political actions and otherwise be involved in civil society organisations. Yet even in the sphere of personal consumption, the zero-waste movement faces issues. For instance, you can still practise a zero-waste lifestyle while flying, as long as you bring your own water bottle and plastic-free snacks with you. Moreover, such movements which primarily target individual consumption do not necessarily focus on some vision of a future, such as a society that exists differently in the world or a worldview which encourages gentleness and care towards the self, others and nature. In fact, attempting to achieve such lifestyles may take the attention of individuals away from political actions, making them focus instead on micromanaging their consumption. Despite these downsides, such movements remain important allies to the degrowth movement. They carry the potential of providing humans with a feeling of being active, of achievement and of hope in the face of ecological degradation. Moreover, since by definition movements such as voluntary simplicity (Elgin and Mitchell 1977) and zero waste deviate from consumerism, being part of them may allow more free time for other activities, such as participating in a community initiative or a trade union or connecting with nature.

On the large scale, civil society organisations may include NGOs and trade unions. One strength of an NGO is already implied in its definition: it is an organisation which operates independently of the government and which thus may be (but not necessarily is) critical of its ideology. In capitalist social formations, NGOs can create spaces for promoting degrowth-compatible ideas and transformations (Burkhart et al. 2020). To give but one example, the degrowth group of environmental NGO Friends of the Earth Denmark arranges seminars and summer schools about degrowth for the public and it makes podcasts and publishes books to increase awareness of what degrowth (in Danish: *modvækst*) is. However, NGOs may also be – and in many cases are – hierarchical and narrowly focused on a particular interest rather than on the deep transformations needed in every domain of societal being. Indeed, today many, if not most, NGOs are embedded in capitalist structures and do not stand in opposition to the growth imperative. In a degrowth society, many of the functions currently performed by NGOs, such as raising awareness and bringing to the surface inequalities and instances of social and ecological degradation, would become societal functions.

As regards unions, they are for the most part married to the idea that a green form of capitalism is possible and desirable. Their proposals of a Green New Deal are underpinned by the notion that it is possible to drastically reduce CO_2 emissions while the economy grows, increasing the number of green jobs. Barca (2019: 212), however, also points to various cases exemplifying that 'there exist, at this historical conjuncture, concrete possibilities for articulating degrowth and labor politics in new ways, via grassroots mobilizations in community unionism and social movement unionism, pushing labor organizations toward a radical critique of the growth paradigm'. While not degrowth oriented, unions can engage in degrowth-compatible struggles. For example, Bieler (2021) analyses how various coalitions between organised workers and other social forces at different scales have effectively waged struggles against the privatisation of water in Europe. The result of many of these struggles against the commodification of the commons have been that water companies have remained publicly owned. Another case is the International Labour Organization's 'just transition' approach: workers in brown industries should be assisted in finding employment in greener sectors through reskilling programmes and financial support. Though originally married to the green growth mainstream, key organisations such as the European Social Observatory and the European Trade Union Institute have started to question the growth paradigm and engage with sustainable welfare and degrowth approaches,[2] linking 'just transition' to these approaches (Sabato et al. 2021).

While trade unions could potentially come to play a role as a force of degrowth transformations, it is important to keep in mind that the political power of this type of civil society organisation has been drastically weakened, as a result of which its past achievements have to some extent been rolled back (Chapter 3). Increasingly, unions 'appear like large but aging dinosaurs struggling to adapt as the climate changes. The proportion of workers who belong to unions is in decline. Centralized systems of wage-setting are breaking apart. Incentive pay schemes and profit-sharing arrangements subvert negotiated wage scales' (Wallerstein and Western 2000: 355). The major unions, then, are far weaker potential allies of the degrowth movement than would have been the case in the heyday of the trade union movement in the 1960s and 1970s. Trade unions in many cases also have shortcomings in addition to those already mentioned. They may be bureaucratic, and they may have greater concern for their own interest as an entity than for the interests of their members (or nature). Here anarchist trade unions may provide an alternative, aimed at 'working with communities rather than trying to take them over or lead them in instrumental manner' (Wilkin and Boudeau 2015: 1338). It is also worth adding that while unions are in decline everywhere, they are stronger in some countries than in others. In the Scandinavian countries in particular, trade unions have better bargaining powers than in countries with liberal forms of capitalism. In the former countries, trade unions would thus be in a relatively better position to contribute to degrowth transformations should they come to be so inclined (Buch-Hansen 2014). For instance, they can advocate for better working conditions, contracts and wages, which would guarantee stability for the workers. Without such stability, it is difficult to imagine that humans would prioritise degrowth transformations.

Civil society organisations are diverse, spanning a wide variety of formal and informal organisation on various scales. Again, seen in relation to degrowth transformations, no particular civil society social form is superior to all others. To give but a few examples of social forms, within academia, groups and networks exist which promote the degrowth discourse as well as broader discourses such as post-growth. Various neighbourhood organisations are compatible with an eco-anarchist vision of degrowth transformations and degrowth society (Trainer 2012, 2014). Such small-scale organisations can contribute to degrowth transformations without waiting for a larger change and the end of capitalism. Organisations of production (see Chapter 6) such as cooperatives, not-for-profit businesses and eco-social enterprises may be, theoretically, at the border between civil society and business. Small-scale organisations of production can provide an answer to the call within the degrowth discourse for more localisations and place-sensitivity (Trainer 2012; Nesterova 2022b).

Multiple online communities which likewise can and do participate in degrowth transformations exist.[3] The issue with such communities is their reliance on technology and the internet. The ever-increasing and intensifying use of technology is problematic for multiple reasons (Heikkurinen 2018). Technology is not neutral; one technology does not exist in isolation from others, the result being the creation of a technological society

(Ruuska and Heikkurinen 2021). Ruuska and Heikkurinen (2021: 13) note that 'the technological world is an atomized and detached world which often leaves people alone and feeling alienated with little or no sense of agency'. A technologically reliant mode of living is difficult to imagine in a world in which energy reduction is pursued: high technology requires energy. Still, some online spaces and organisations can indeed be helpful for transformations towards degrowth, for instance, in terms of organising political actions for degrowth transformations, sharing knowledge, and making more effective redistribution of existing goods and services possible. Currently, many initiatives which target waste reduction and redistribution are based on high technology. For instance, initiatives such as REKO rings (Hushållningssällskapet 2022), where producers and consumers come together without intermediaries, require the use of technology: they connect most often via a popular social media website. Payment is likewise done using apps.

It is important to stress that while no social form is 'the best' in relation to degrowth transformations, individuals are different and as such they will always be attracted to different types of civil society organisation depending on personal worldviews and political commitments (that is, provided they are at all attracted to such social forms). For instance, adherents of individualist anarchism or anarcho-primitivism are unlikely to be drawn to formal, bureaucratic and hierarchical organisations. For the adherents of socialism as a political ideology for a degrowth society, formal organisations such as trade unions may be more acceptable.

State policies can support civil society organisations, placing them in a better position to become driving forces in degrowth transformations. Owing to the wide variety of forms taken by civil society organisations, a diverse range of policies could be implemented to this end. Many civil society organisations operate on a voluntary basis. People who contribute their time, energy and skills are often not paid for their efforts. This excludes many individuals from participation. A suitable policy to increase participation in various civil society organisations is the provision of a universal basic income or universal basic services: without reliance on a job and an income, at least partially, people can familiarise themselves with the range of civil society organisations they can get involved with, or dedicate more time to the ones they are already part of. Apart from the universal basic income, increasing monetary support is required for multiple civil society organisations. For instance, this applies to NGOs, academic groups and networks involved in researching degrowth transformations, community initiatives and neighbourhood groups. Some organisations, such as those involved in the production of food, require policies which support access to land.

Individuals and their self-transformations

In discussing civil society as something singular (for example, as a site or an entity), it should be remembered that civil society, and everything within it, emerges from and through the causal powers and actions of individual human beings (Danermark et al. 2002). For their existence and operations, as well as their reproduction and transformation, organisations within civil society likewise rely on the involvement of individuals.

While placing causal powers within the domain of human agency, theorising human beings is essential. Otherwise, it may be asked, what lets us assume that civil society members would take part in transformations? First and foremost, it is important to reject the notion of a human being as a rational utility maximiser, otherwise known as the 'economic man' of neoclassical economics. It is difficult to imagine that degrowth transformations can be carried out by humans if humans are greedy, egocentric and narrowly self-interested (Chapter 1). It is likewise difficult to pursue degrowth transformations if such ideas of humans are promoted in society, such as in the system of education. After all, the 'way in which we think of ourselves – the picture we form of our essential nature – directly affects the way we live' (Midgley 2003: xvi). Neoclassical economics is notorious for misrepresenting human nature (Bhaskar 1998; Eskelinen and Wilen 2019; Gills and Morgan 2021; Lawson 2019; Schumacher 1993; Söderbaum 2008). In this school of thought, humans are reduced to materialistic and egocentric beings (Bhaskar 1998; Lawson 2015; Söderbaum 2008; Spash 2017). Even if human beings exhibit such characteristics, in reality they are much more complex than that (see Chapter 7). Moreover, human beings are always in the process of evolution, becoming and growing. That is, the self of humans is more akin to a journey than to a fixed entity (Polkinghorne 2015). Thus, instead of assuming that a human being is an 'economic man' with one or a few particular attributes (Lawson 2019), the notion of a real, unique, relational and complex human being, capable of transforming the world around her/himself as well as being capable of self-transformation, should be embraced. Seeing humans this way is not unusual. For instance, it is a feature of some strands of heterodox economics (Becker 2006; Spash 2012) as well as neighbouring sciences and humanities such as human geography (Tuan 1974, 1998), philosophy (Bhaskar 2012a) and psychology (Schneider et al. 2015).

Excluding 'economic man' as a member of civil society means looking into other disciplines which may assist in understanding who the members of civil society are. Human nature has traditionally been a major focus for philosophy and psychology (Boss 1988). In terms of philosophy, critical realism and existentialism may be helpful in understanding humans in relation to degrowth transformations (Heikkurinen 2018; Nesterova 2021c). The philosophy of metaReality (Bhaskar 2012c), which is the continuation of Bhaskar's original philosophy of critical realism (Bhaskar 1989, 1998), has in recent times also become a feature of the degrowth literature landscape (e.g., Buch-Hansen and Nesterova 2021, 2023; Nesterova 2021c). Critical realism assumes that agents have causal powers and the ability to act on the world, including themselves (Buch-Hansen and Nielsen 2020; Collier 2003; Danermark et al. 2002). A better society is possible via this causation and human qualities (Nesterova 2021b). Critical realists contend that humans are naturally concerned about the state of the world around them (Sayer 2011) and are inherently capable of love, fellow-feeling, care, empathy, creativity and freedom (Bhaskar 2012a, 2012b). Love in this case does not simply refer to a feeling towards a particular individual. Rather, it signifies an overarching sense of interdependence and togetherness (Bhaskar 2012b). Naturally, being capable of something (such as fellow-feeling and care) does not mean that these qualities do not require nurturing. Indeed, wars, violence and exploitation provide evidence of humans being capable of suppressing or not exercising their humane capacities.

Existentialist philosophers whose works provided inspiration within the degrowth field include, for instance, Albert Camus and Martin Heidegger. Existentialist philosophy conceptually places humans into a concrete, but imperfect and complicated world (Boss 1988; Heidegger 2001; Sartre 2000). That is, while human nature itself is contentious, our being in and dwelling (belonging) in concrete locations and places is something that cannot be denied. This means that humans are always subject to certain natural and social structures such as topographies and social, cultural and political systems (Buch-Hansen 2014; Hägerstrand 2012). Humans' experiences, circumstances and possibilities for actions differ depending on the constellation of structures within which they exist.

Existentialism views humans as embodied, that is, having a real, physical presence in the natural and the social worlds (Heidegger 2001; van Deurzen and Adams 2016). Being part of the social world means that even though humans are singular and unique, we are always co-present with other humans. Existentialism structures human existence around three or even four dimensions, hence presenting humans as relational beings. These relations concern the environment (*Umwelt*), the social dimension (*Mitwelt*) and the personal dimension (*Eigenwelt*) (Heidegger 2001; van Deurzen and Adams 2016). The spiritual dimension (*Überwelt*) can also be included (van Deurzen and Adams 2016). The nature of every person's embeddedness in each and all of those dimensions or worlds is different, as is the experience of humans even within the same structures. For degrowth to come into being, transformations need to occur in each of these dimensions. That is to say that humans need to transform their relationship with the environment, within society and with themselves.

While navigating these dimensions or worlds, each human being infuses their own life with meaning (Camus 2005). Seeking meaning may be the core function of human consciousness (Frankl 2006). The meaning a human assigns to their own life and relationships within each of these worlds may direct their behaviour and the mode of being in the world. Under capitalism, the meaning of human existence tends to be reduced to the accumulation of material wealth. Yet various perspectives exist that are better aligned with human qualities and that emphasise genuine human experiences over materialism. This is reflected, for instance, in the mode of being of Erich Fromm. As noted in Chapter 1, Fromm (2013) identifies two modes in which a human being can be: the mode of having and the mode of being. The mode of having focuses on possessions, profit, status and the material. This mode is characterised by a utilitarian position towards nature, others and the self, that is, the self is imagined as a tool for achievement of status. In this mode, the engagement of humans with civil society organisations may be inauthentic and driven by the pursuit of status or material/financial benefits for example, rather than human emancipation, care and harmonious coexistence with nature. For instance, one may join a trade union for one's own benefits rather than as a political act aimed at human emancipation.

The mode of being, conversely, is the mode of authentic existence, where empathy, solidarity and generosity are nurtured and thrive. To live in this mode 'means to renew oneself, to grow, to flow out, to love, to transcend the prison of one's isolated ego, to be interested, … to give' (Fromm 2013: 76). In the mode of being, private property and having more generally is of little importance inasmuch as ownership is not the prerequisite for being able to use and enjoy something. As Fromm (2013: 99) writes, 'Nothing unites people more (without restricting their individuality) than sharing their admiration and love for a person; sharing an idea, a piece of music, a painting, a symbol; sharing in a ritual – and sharing sorrow.'

While it is important that humans step onto the path of being rather than having, it is likewise important to recognise the uniqueness of everyone's journey. In placing much value and hope in cooperation (e.g., Trainer 2012), the degrowth discourse overlooks the needs and inclinations of those who, while remaining part of the civil society, may not desire to organise with others (Nesterova 2022b). For instance, such individuals may find value in solitude and connectedness with the wider community of life (e.g., Thoreau 2016) and not necessarily strive to be part of formal organisations with their fellow humans. Adherents of deep ecology (Næss 2016) attempt to nurture fellow-feeling towards other beings beyond humans (Diehm 2007). This, by definition, widens one's circle of connection and relationships. Trees, mountains, rivers and lakes, as well as other beings and features of nature, become morally and relationally significant. This may encourage individuals to seek to spend more time in and with nature, adopt an outdoors-based lifestyle, live in a sparsely populated or rural area and practise self-sufficiency.

This does not necessarily indicate withdrawal from society (this indeed would be impossible), but rather expanding the notion of who one's fellow beings are far beyond humans. For such individuals, a more isolated mode of being or small eco-communities may be suitable. While such individuals may be in the minority (Leopold 1949), they still should be accounted for in the degrowth discourse. Apart from such cases of individuals who find the sense of connectedness and belonging in the wider community of life, others, due to their personalities, worldviews or ideological commitments, may actively strive to organise and participate in social forms in civil society such as social groups, charities, NGOs, trade unions and others.

In conclusion

In this chapter we have considered civil society in degrowth transformations. We conceptualised civil society as a site and force of transformations, noting that it constitutes a space where diverse and multiple transformations occur and in which a large variety of social forms (organisations, networks etc.) exist through which individuals can work collectively to pursue different kinds and degrees of transformation. The chapter also reflected on the scales and diversity of civil society, noting that degrowth transformations would require agency spanning multiple scales and social forms. Finally, further to the importance we ascribe to individuals in our consideration of civil society, we highlighted the importance of self-transformation. We include individuals in our contemplation of civil society because neither can civil society exist without individuals reproducing it individually and collectively (Bhaskar 1998), nor is any individual unaffected by civil society. The same observations can be made about the state and businesses, and for this reason we also touch upon individual self-transformation in these sites in the following two chapters. Still, we decided to devote particular attention to the matter in the present chapter for the simple reason that whereas individuals positioned in those other sites are members of civil society, the reverse is not necessarily the case.

Activism for degrowth may take very different forms in civil society and thus needs to be understood in broad terms. It does not need to be limited to participating in political campaigns, protests or strikes. It can take more personal and subtle, but still important, forms such as adopting different lifestyles and modes of being, creating music, poetry and art, and different approaches to teaching and knowledge sharing. Despite the focus on the 'self' in self-transformations, the journey and the acts of self-transformations are a social practice since one is always an inseparable part of society. Self-transformation is at its core an activity whose ultimate aim is to create a better world while realising that one's agency is the best place to start. In this sense, self-transformation is a form of activism for degrowth. Since self-transformation requires and entails personal growth, it may enhance self-knowledge (Neisser 1988) and thus help the person to identify the other kinds of activism that, apart from self-transformation, are best suited for them as a unique human being.

Notes

1 Whereas in its modern use civil society is different from the state, it was synonymous with the state or political society up until the end of the eighteenth century (Kumar 1993). In Aristotle's thinking, for example, civil society is synonymous with the ruling elites of the polis, the Athenian civic community.
2 An example is the commissioning of a chapter on 'Sustainable welfare, degrowth and eco-social policies in Europe' in the annual publication *Social Policy in European Union: State of Play* (Koch 2018b).
3 Schmelzer et al. (2022: 217) discuss Wikipedia as a case of global commoning: The world's largest encyclopaedia developed on the grounds of 'contribution rather than exchange'.

5

The state in degrowth transformations

In green political thought, including degrowth thought, it is not uncommon to see the state as part of the problem rather than the solution (Gough 2017). Nevertheless, most of the eco-social policies that are typically suggested to initiate and deepen degrowth transformations – be it in relation to respecting ecological ceilings or social floors (Khan et al. 2022; see Chapter 7) – would require a great deal of intervention by states and/or international organisations (Cosme et al. 2017). Degrowth advocacy has therefore suffered from a tension between viewing the state as incapable of initiating transformational change and appealing to it to do precisely that. This tension has, on occasion, taken the form of passionate arguments between 'state-orientated' and 'state-opposed' (often anarchist) degrowth advocates such as during the 2018 6th International Degrowth Conference in Malmö. In the present chapter, we seek to overcome the tension via a broad theoretical perspective on the state, a key institutional form (Chapter 2). We first analyse the state's roles in the capitalist growth economy, focusing for instance on the welfare and the environmental state. Subsequently, we turn to the potential role of the state in degrowth transformations, considering the form and scales of state intervention, as well as its content in terms of sustainable welfare and eco-social policies.

State roles in capitalist growth economies

In developing our perspective, we draw on recent degrowth scholarship which has started to reconcile state-orientated and state-opposed thinking through a rereading of some classics of state theory (Koch 2020a, 2022a; see also D'Alisa and Kallis 2020 and Görg et al. 2017). Koch unifies the state theories of Gramsci (1971), Poulantzas (1978) and Bourdieu (2014). The three understand the state in relation to wider society, while theorising corresponding patterns of dominance and subordination. They also bring together the two most established social science traditions on the subject, namely the Marxian and the Weberian traditions. Whereas the Marxist tradition emphasises the interconnection of state policies and the capitalist growth imperative, the Weberian tradition focuses on the socio-historic processes that led to the modern bureaucratic state. The three theorists are furthermore united in viewing the state as a relatively autonomous sphere where dominating and dominated groups represent and struggle for their interests. Accordingly, existing state policies do not reflect the interests of any single group of actors. Rather they are outcomes of compromises between social forces within and beyond the state apparatus.

In capitalism, processes of production and wealth creation are structurally separated from the political processes of exercising coercive power and administrative control. Marx, in particular, linked the autonomous existence of the state to the structural prerequisites of the market economy. To be able to exchange goods, individuals must 'recognize one another reciprocally as proprietors' (Marx 1973: 243). The state legally facilitates such exchanges, guaranteeing the legal and economic independence of the owners of commodities, preventing, for instance, the appropriation of commodities by force. In this context, the modern state constitutes an independent third party that monopolises the legitimate use of physical force (Weber 1991: 78).

Complementing this perspective, Bourdieu introduced the notion of the state as the monopoly of legitimate symbolic violence. Like Gramsci's concept of hegemony, symbolic capital is the power of making people see the world in a specific way, which, if this power is sufficiently strong, appears as the only possible, universal and natural way. This manifests itself, for instance, in the state's power to judge sentences and regulate the rules of spelling. More than merely shaping peoples' consciousness, symbolic domination entails bodily aspects being submitted to (state) power (Bourdieu 1994, 2014). State power, then, takes on both physical and symbolic forms. Because of the strength of symbolic power, the state rarely has to resort to the use of physical force (Bourdieu 2014: 166). Bourdieu understands state power as the historical process of concentration of different forms of capital (including physical force and economic, cultural, informational and symbolic capital). The state is itself a field like others with oppositions such as that between its 'left hand' (public education, health and social welfare) and 'right hand' (judiciary, domestic affairs and finance departments). However, unlike other fields, the state transcends different forms of capital and has historically played an important role in differentiating civil society into fields (Chapter 4). With his notion of the 'integral state', which combines political (the formal state apparatus) and civil society, Gramsci (1971) addresses a similar topic: that contemporary states and civil societies are interlinked in myriad ways, making them empirically difficult to keep apart.

Symbolic state power becomes embodied and fixed in dispositions and habits (what Bourdieu refers to as 'habitus', see Chapter 7) and affects the various planes of social being. For example, the school system and other state institutions often reinforce the view of extractivism as the one and only possible form of human transaction with nature, and utilitarianism as the only form of interaction between humans. Nature is here seen as a 'free gift' for (economic) capital expansion, and other humans as means to materialist ends. Capitalist state institutions expose citizens to the ideal of 'economic man' and the corresponding values of competitiveness, individual advancement and short-term gain, paired often with intolerance, racism, sexism and a general hate of everything and everyone presumed to be different and 'other'. Further to this, the symbolic power of the capitalist state shapes peoples' inner being in the direction of entitlement, materialism and egoism.

In a social formation based on exploitative and exclusionary relationships, pertaining for instance to class, race, religion and gender (Chapter 1), the state is the main location for the political regulation of conflicts and for the maintenance of social order (Offe 1984). Since society risks disintegration without such regulation, states ensure the maintenance of a minimum of social cohesion and, at the same time, the legitimisation of remaining inequalities. For example, countless sociological studies since Bourdieu and Passeron (1977) have shown that the existing school system largely reproduces and reinforces inherited inequalities, that is, the children's original social differences. Not least by mystifying and naturalising such differences, the state has proven quite capable of temporarily harmonising conflicting group interests. Still, state policies do not normally simply follow the interests of dominant classes and groups; they also reflect the interests of the dominated ones to some extent. Specific state structures and activities, as well as corresponding modes of governance, are linked to 'social forces, practices and discourses, the (changing) societal context as well as the contested functions or tasks of the state in societal reproduction', including that of 'existing societal nature relations' (Görg et al. 2017: 9).

The state constitutes a relatively autonomous political sphere, where social classes and groups represent their interests in indirect and mediated ways. As political parties and civil society groups raise various issues, they sometimes become the focus of government action, only to be superseded by others at later points in time. State policies develop, then, as results of the heterogeneity and changing dynamic of social forces that influence state institutions (Jessop 2002). Once such a coalition of relatively powerful actors has been formed and has managed to influence the general direction of state policies, it takes on the character of a relatively homogeneous social force. The more socially coherent the coalition of forces that influences the state is, the less the contradictions there will be across state policies. Gramsci and Poulantzas referred to such a coalition of groups capable of temporarily dominating state policies as a 'power bloc' (akin to what was called a 'historic bloc' in Chapter 3). To underline the state's role in securing and stabilising wider societal relations and various social struggles and power asymmetries, Poulantzas (1978) used the term 'condensation'. The state, then, is a powerful actor which itself is created and recreated by social forces.

On the one hand, the state facilitates the stabilisation and maintenance of the social order via its force, laws, regulations, curricula, resources and its discourses of legitimation. On the other hand, however, concrete state strategies are the results of the material and symbolic struggles and tensions between social forces within and beyond its institutional borders, which may take the form of contradictions between different state apparatuses and branches. Different state apparatuses may, in fact, address problems in different ways. For instance, while one may promote growth and the use of fossil energy, another may attempt to reduce carbon emissions by reducing the use of fossil energy (Brand et al. 2011). Social movements can potentially use such contradictions within the state to advance their interests and turn their projects into hegemonic ones (Görg et al. 2017; Poulantzas 1978).

The post-Second World War welfare state resulted from struggles between organised labour and capital as well as between factions within the wider state apparatus. This Western welfare state defined the extent to which labour power is 'decommodified' (Esping-Andersen 1990). Subsequent work in comparative social policy was dedicated to national divisions of labour between markets, states and the third sector, taking the institutional forms of 'welfare regimes' (Arts and Gelissen 2002). It pointed to how the social-democratic countries in Northern Europe traditionally featured greater amounts of equality than did liberal (such as the UK) or conservative (such as Germany) countries.

A further landmark step in the internal differentiation process of the state in advanced capitalist countries has been the establishment of the environmental state (Chapter 2). Paralleling the development of the welfare state, the creation of the environmental state can be traced back to struggles between environmental groups and initiatives against large business and state interests. Duit et al. (2016: 5) define the environmental state as a 'set of institutions and practices dedicated to the management of the environment and societal-environmental interactions'. In addition to being a provider of welfare to a smaller or larger extent, then, contemporary states in some respects protect nature. In other respects they simultaneously allow for violence being done to nature and in some cases states directly cause it themselves. For example, some of the world's largest oil companies are state owned (Babić 2023). Just as in the case of the welfare state, the expansion of the environmental state is not a linear and uncontested development.

A recent example of a drawback of the environmental state is the right-wing populist Swedish government abolishing the environmental ministry as an independent department.

Recent scholarship explored the similarities and differences in the historical developments and current roles of welfare and environmental states. It found that their institutional, political and economic contexts differ significantly, as does the composition of supporting and opposing social groupings and associated constellations (Gough 2016). Esping-Andersen's welfare regime approach has inspired debates on the environmental state. According to Dryzek et al. (2003), for example, social-democratic welfare states are better placed to manage the intersection of social and environmental policies than are liberal market economies and welfare regimes. Social-democratic welfare regimes generally make a conscious and coordinated effort to manage this intersection and regard economic and ecological values as mutually reinforcing (Gough et al. 2008). Yet, although these regimes are the most equal ones in socio-economic terms, their ecological performance is not superior (Koch and Fritz 2014; Duit 2016; Jakobsson et al. 2018). Rather, roughly speaking, the richer a country the worse its environmental performance (Fritz and Koch 2016; O'Neill et al. 2018).

State regulation is permanently subject to rescaling processes resulting in new, multi-scalar structures of state organisation and socio-economic regulation operating on different scales (Kazepov 2010). Particular capitalist growth regimes are oriented towards different scales. The Fordist growth model, for example, focused on the national level. Eventually, it came under pressure through various processes of rescaling and deregulation. In this process, powers were delegated from the national state apparatus to other scales, such as the subnational, regional and transnational ones (Jessop 2002: 206). Increasingly, transnational processes of capital accumulation require regulation extending beyond the borders and capacities of individual states. On the one hand, this led governments to create and strengthen regional and global regulatory systems and institutions such as the EU, the World Bank and the IMF. On the other hand, in the neoliberal era, transnational class actors and institutions have become significant sources of domestic policy ideas and design, and implementation. The contemporary international regulatory sphere constitutes a 'multi-scalar and poly-centred system of governance', where states and international organisations interact, albeit not on equal terms (Ougaard 2018: 129). Up until now the interests of the rich countries have largely managed to define the rules of this international regulatory sphere (Castree 2008; Brand and Wissen 2013; Hickel 2020).

Scales and diversity of degrowth transformations

We now turn to the potential role played by the state in degrowth trans-formations. As in previous chapters, what is provided here is not a precise blueprint. Indeed, no serious treatment of degrowth can deliver this. What is offered instead is a broader framework for thinking about the state in degrowth transformations, which builds on the previous section and our reflections in Chapter 2 on the 'degrowth state' as an institutional form. In what follows, we first consider issues related to scale and form, and then focus on content by turning to the notion of sustainable welfare and the eco-social policies that are currently being discussed in degrowth circles.

Many degrowth thinkers advocate strong localist visions (Trainer 2012) and in this context regard municipalities as key change agents. They envi-sion international networks of towns and cities as driving forces behind transformations. The local 'scale of politics is considered ideal for degrowth as it is in the municipality that people can practise face-to-face political deliberation' (Schmelzer et al. 2022: 249).[1] As regards the state, it is per-ceived mainly as a negative force which is, for instance, disrupting the neces-sary transformations, maintaining borders and acting in authoritarian ways (2022: 291). In this view, then, there is little room for national states to play a positive role in degrowth transformations. Such transformations are, it would seem, mainly to be driven by actors in other sites or state appara-tuses on other scales. Our take on degrowth transformations is somewhat different, in that we find it difficult to imagine how such transformations could ever come to enjoy the necessary momentum on a societal scale in the absence of comprehensive state involvement. This is not to turn a blind eye to the negative aspects of contemporary state activities or to say that we see the state as *the* key actor in degrowth transformations; it is to say that we see national state policies as one very important mechanism that, alongside action at the local and transnational levels, can facilitate such transformations.

Further to the observations in the previous sections, it should be recog-nised that degrowth processes unfold from the starting point of a regula-tory architecture that spans several scales. State apparatuses existing on the local, national and transnational scales may act to block transformations, but potentially they could also come to play more positive roles. In our per-spective, primacy should not be ascribed to state interventions on any one particular scale. Rather, state activities on various scales are important to degrowth transformations. Importantly, on each scale, the state would have different *functions*.

On the *national scale*, the state has a key role to play as a provider of 'sustainable welfare' (a matter we come back to in the next section) and more generally as an actor initiating a host of degrowth-compatible reforms and other activities in collaboration with civil society actors and businesses to ensure the respect of ecological and social limits in production and consumption patterns. Most eco-social policies, including, for instance, a reduction in working hours, most taxation and many green finance initiatives, would seem suitable for this scale. State power can also be used to build transnational networks connecting myriad local economies.

As regards the *transnational scale*, interstate collaboration would be important, for instance in the context of international bodies such as the United Nations, the OECD and the EU. Just as the capitalist national state would need to gradually be transformed into a degrowth state in order to come to play a positive role in the transition, international organisations – the bulk of which currently (at best) promote 'green growth' – would also need to be profoundly reformed. One reason the transnational scale is important in relation to degrowth transformations is that it is the scale at which local and national policies can be coordinated. Such coordination is crucial inasmuch as the adoption of a particular degrowth-compatible policy, say a tax on pollution, in one country may have no or detrimental effects if other countries introduce no such tax. In a similar vein, if a policy such as caps on income and wealth is not to result in capital flight on a major scale, it would either need to be implemented directly by international organisations or, if implemented by national states, be closely coordinated at the transnational level (Buch-Hansen and Koch 2019). Sustainable welfare, for instance, entails that some of the distributive principles underlying existing OECD welfare systems are extended to include people living in other countries and into the future (Brandstedt and Emmelin 2016). To make this happen, cooperation at the transnational scale would undoubtedly also be required.

It would also be important for the degrowth state to delegate powers to the *local scale*. This is the scale at which direct participatory democracy (complementing representative democracy) is most feasible and the scale at which degrowth initiatives tailored to local circumstances can be launched. As such it is a crucial scale. A range of eco-social policies may well be implemented at the local level, cases in point being policies related to funding of local degrowth-compatible businesses, many educational activities, transportation and housing provision.

In proposing that state action at multiple scales is important to degrowth transformations (see also Moore et al. 2014), and in linking the scales with particular eco-social policies, we do not mean to suggest that the relative importance of state activities at different scales would not vary over time and geographically. As regards the temporal aspect, it is conceivable that state action at the national level would be more important in early stages of degrowth transformations than later on. An example would be nationalising the currently enormous fossil energy sector as a precondition to a quick phase-out of the burning of oil, gas and coal[2] to retain any chance of meeting the Paris climate targets.[3] As a corollary, the state's wealth and power would increase in an initial phase, only to decrease again in sync with the disappearance of fossil energy extraction and the concomitant transition to renewable energy sources and their communalisation/localisation in a second phase. Smaller states may be acceptable as long as these are embedded in an economic system that provides relatively egalitarian outcomes and costs related to inequality, (unhealthy) work-life balances and environmental deterioration. During the transition, state policies would be indispensable to steer just transitions for those currently employed in the fossil fuel industries (Chapter 4). In the long term, the involvement of the state may be essential in safely handling technologically complex and expensive operations, such as management of nuclear waste, which cannot be handled by local communities.

In terms of geography, it is important to keep in mind that transformations start out from currently existing institutional arrangements, arrangements that vary considerably from one place to the next. That is, further to the observations regarding capitalist diversity and the importance of existing institutions to degrowth transformations that were made in Chapter 2, divergent non-identical driving forces are likely to initiate degrowth transformations in different countries, transformations that start out from different forms of capitalism. Keeping things simple, we can distinguish between three varieties of capitalism: a liberal, a state-led and a coordinated variety (Chapter 4; see also Buch-Hansen 2014). Countries currently characterised by the market-oriented *liberal form of capitalism* such as the UK, the US and Australia are premised on the view that competitive relations between businesses are essential to maximising wealth in society. The state generally does not intervene directly in markets but sets rules and settles conflicts. In such countries a broad movement in civil society initiating the transformation itself is a more likely scenario than it is that the state or a coalition of social forces cutting across the traditional class divide would initiate it.

Countries with *state-led capitalism*, in which the state, for example, intervenes in market relations to steer business development, is where the prospects of centrally steered initiations of degrowth transformations are most likely. Cases in point, at least in some respects, are France, Japan, Russia and China. State-led degrowth transformations are most likely in countries with strong social and intellectual movements that support these transformations and provide inputs to them. Thus, of the countries just mentioned, France is the more likely candidate to witness this sort of degrowth trajectory. In countries with *coordinated capitalism*, in which business relationships tend to be coordinated and network-based, the state typically does not intervene directly in the market. In such countries – the Scandinavian countries and Germany being cases in point – degrowth transformations could conceivably be initiated via broad societal compromise between governments and employers' associations and unions, perhaps in alliance with various interest groups and social movements, such as the environmental movement.[4]

Our point is not to suggest that the degrowth trajectories just outlined are currently the most likely scenarios to unfold in the various types of capitalism (it follows from the argument in Chapter 3 that degrowth transformations are currently not very likely to happen on a societal scale). Rather, the point is that in some contexts, the national state is more likely to play a prominent role in facilitating such transformations than in others. Because of the diversity of the institutional frameworks in different types of capitalism, and because degrowth transformations would materialise through open-ended democratic processes, degrowth would take different forms in different settings.

Sustainable welfare, eco-social policies and self-transformations

The matter and energy throughput, and the associated ecological footprint of global society would need to shrink if it is to respect ecological limits. This concerns, above all, the rich countries, yet the populations of many developing countries also already live beyond their ecological means (Fritz and Koch 2016). Reduction of humanity's ecological footprint, however, is not the end in itself to be achieved by any means possible. It should come together with the satisfaction of the basic needs of all. To pursue the achievement of this dual aim, several frameworks conceptualise a 'space' where ecological and social considerations meet (Rockström et al. 2009; Raworth 2017). Ecological considerations would ensure that the use of nature's resources is below the level of planetary limits, while social considerations establish social boundaries whereby basic needs (but not hedonic wants) of all humans are satisfied. This resonates with the calls for 'sustainable welfare', which combines social welfare approaches with sustainability beyond economic growth (Koch and Mont 2016).

The satisfaction of human needs rather than hedonic wants is central both to sustainable welfare and degrowth (Koch et al. 2017; Büchs and Koch 2019).[5] Needs differ from wants in that they are non-negotiable and universal (that is, they do not vary over time and across cultures) and that failure to satisfy these produces serious harm (Gough 2017). While needs are universal, how they are satisfied varies geo-historically (Max-Neef 1991; see also Chapter 7 for an empirical operationalisation based on a combination of academic/codified and practical knowledge). For instance, the need for food or subsistence was satisfied by hunter-gatherer communities via foraging, while the same need is most often satisfied by modern societies via global, industrial production and distribution of food mediated by money.

To achieve the satisfaction of the basic needs of all humans while staying within the ecological limits of the planet, corresponding policies need to be introduced. In the literature, state policies are frequently highlighted as mechanisms of key importance to bring about degrowth (e.g., Fitzpatrick et al. 2022). Many of the discussed policies are *eco-social* policies, that is, policies advancing at once ecological and social goals (Dukelow and Murphy 2022; Gough 2017). For example, slow travel by train may be less affordable than flying and thus unaffordable to many. As a result, many people fly. Subsidising train tickets can thus simultaneously serve the purpose of making transportation affordable to all as well as reducing the environmental impact of transportation. Caps on income and wealth, and income and wealth taxes, are likewise eco-social policies. They can at the same time reduce economic inequality via redistribution and prevent rich individuals from overconsuming and leading environmentally unsustainable lifestyles (Pizzigati 2018).

To ensure that the basic needs of all are satisfied, suggestions have been made for the introduction of a universal and unconditional basic income (e.g., van Parijs and Vanderborght 2017), the expansion/introduction of universal basic services such as housing, education, healthcare and transportation (e.g., Coote and Percy 2020), a voucher system (Bohnenberger 2020), or a combination of these policies (Büchs 2021). Implementation of such policies is an expensive undertaking which can initially be financed via greater taxation of wealth or caps on income and/or wealth. Proposals to place a cap on income usually suggest some quantitative proportion to minimum incomes such as 10:1 or 20:1 (Concialdi 2018; Martin et al. 2023). Beyond this, 100% taxation would take place. There is, however, no agreement about where exactly the cap level should be set and which forms of wealth should be targeted (Buch-Hansen and Koch 2019). Beyond suggesting income caps and wealth taxation as the policies which target the ecological aspects of consumption, other ecological policies include decarbonisation of energy supply, carbon rationing and protecting nature and the commons from the interests of multinational corporations (Büchs and Koch 2017).

Some policies target the quality of life and wellbeing beyond the satisfaction of basic needs. Working time reduction is an example of such a policy (Spencer 2022). Reduction of working time, combined with the reassurance that basic needs of a person are (and will be) satisfied, can free up time for engaging in, for instance, activism, spiritual pursuits and education. Education in itself is a sphere in need of reform. Currently, it is often the case that instrumental views of nature and other humans are promoted by the education system. Employability, or becoming appealing and useful to someone else's pursuits of profit, rather than personal growth and responsibility towards the self, others and nature, is highlighted. Starting from the very first stages of formal education, environmental and social values need to be nurtured. This concerns the content of curricula as well as teaching spaces, forms and methods. For instance, nature- and art-based didactical traditions can be utilised alongside more traditional, classroom-based modes of interaction between teachers and students (Huizinga 1950; Macy and Johnstone 2022).

It is important to note that the policies identified above should not be seen in isolation from one another. No single policy can bring about degrowth transformation on its own. For instance, it may be unaffordable for governments to implement a universal basic income without wealth taxation in the longer term. Changing school curricula without reforming the labour market and creating space for a different way of running business (see Chapter 6) can create a mismatch between the graduates' skills and employers' desires. Enforcing carbon and income caps and thus reducing the possibilities for consumption would only result in frustration if humans are not encouraged to relate to the self, others and nature differently from the beginning of their life.

The challenge to implementing such policies is not a lack of knowledge about them or a lack of ideas. Yet, as mentioned, financing of a programme including a multitude, if not all, the policies identified above, would be enormously expensive. In the absence of GDP growth it is very likely that rich countries would experience tax losses despite the new sources of income deriving from, for instance, the taxation of wealth (Bailey 2015: 795). Combining sustainable welfare and deviation from GDP growth thus remains a challenge (Büchs 2021; Koch 2022b). One way to make financing easier is a new transnationally coordinated system of taxation which requires cooperation and solidarity between nations. Here, national governments would need to play active roles in achieving this new tax system and consider the interests of humanity as a whole rather than the interests of one's own nation. The issue of financing comes with another challenge, that of orchestrating the eco-social policy cycle, that is, combining these policies in such a way which will result in synergies and ultimately in all humans' needs being satisfied sufficiently and sustainably within nature's limits (see e.g., Hirvilammi 2020).

In orchestrating the eco-social policy cycle, it is important to avoid glamorising these policies by assuming a direct and immediate link between their implementation and human wellbeing. It may well be that the process of implementation would be riddled with difficulties. Moreover, though basic human needs can presumably be met during the transition, many individuals may experience decreased subjective wellbeing, at least in the short term (Koch et al. 2017). Eco-social policies will significantly alter humans' way of life. Though the current way of life is not ecologically sustainable or solidaric, it is familiar. Stepping on a different path may cause anxiety, fear and ultimately search for a new meaning (Frankl 2006) and one's place in the world. Only if members of civil society self-transform are they likely to embrace a fundamentally different way of life. Importantly, the need for self-transformation applies well beyond civil society. Although it has unfortunately so far barely been recognised in the degrowth discourse, the role of the state regarding self-transformations is not limited to facilitating such transformation of the 'subjects' of the state (members of the civil society). It also includes nurturing self-transformations in individuals positioned within state apparatuses, including, for instance, politicians, judges and administrators.[6]

Currently, the green growth discourse continues to shape the worldviews and hence policymaking of many of these individuals – that is, provided any ecological and social reflections arise at all, which may typically not be the case with respect to, for instance, law enforcement and military personnel. Self-transformations of the state 'from within' entail largely the same self-transformations that would need to unfold in all the other members of society. As we have already discussed this in some detail in Chapter 4, suffice it to say that self-transformations would entail reflecting on one's being part of the broader natural and social world. This reflection would involve acting in and upon the world correspondingly, with genuine concern and with immaterial values such as love, friendship, care, fellow-feeling, solidarity and empathy guiding one's actions.

Such self-transformation 'from within' the state is necessary if the emergence of new state nobilities, that is, occupants of power positions in various government and administrative departments, is to be prevented. Even state philosophies (such as social democracy and communism) which claimed to have broad human interests in mind repeatedly led to the emergence of new state nobilities. Rather than tackling ecological and social issues, such individuals and their groups focused on defending their power against competing groups within the state bureaucracy. While the degrowth discourse insists on its inherent difference from other approaches and its genuine concern for all humans and nature, it is not immune to a similar unfolding of power relations. Discussions on how the focus on power can be discouraged beyond the call for self-transformations are important. Proposals may include limiting public office to a certain number of years and complementing the institutions of representative democracy with the elements of direct democracy.

In conclusion

In this chapter we have outlined a broad theoretical perspective on the state and used it to shed light on the state's role both in capitalist social formations and in degrowth transformations. Our perspective, which seeks to transcend state-oriented and state-opposed thinking, entails viewing the state and civil society as strongly interconnected. Consequently, state policy is regarded as fundamentally shaped by social forces within and beyond the state. In this view, the state could come to play a positive – indeed crucial – role in degrowth transformations if a comprehensive coalition of social forces (a power bloc) united around the political project of degrowth were to gain sufficient momentum. The state can play an important role in facilitating self-transformations in civil society and business, yet it is equally important that such transformations occur within the individuals occupying positions in the state itself. It also follows from this perspective that any strategy for degrowth exclusively targeting civil society and not the state (or vice versa) is unlikely to be successful (Koch 2022a).

What, then, are the main differences between the capitalist state and the degrowth state? In capitalist circumstances, the growth paradigm delineates the limits for state action in economic, social and environmental domains to a significant extent. Environmental policies are feasible only so long as these do not undermine the overall growth orientation. Hence, state action is largely reduced to the facilitation of 'green growth'. In a degrowth context, by contrast, the policy priority of achieving economic growth is replaced by the goal of moving the economy and society into a space where both ecological and social considerations are met. The economic, social and environmental policies of the state would be oriented towards minimising matter and energy throughput and maximising sustainable welfare, specifically the provision of sufficient need satisfiers for all people now and in the future. Another difference pertains to the nature of steering: although degrowth would probably require many policies oriented towards the national scale as well as transnational coordination, substantial powers would be delegated from the national to the local scale, where citizens can shape policies through direct participation.

Thinking about how different kinds of eco-social policies may be combined to initiate a new virtuous circle of policymaking in degrowth contexts is important (Hirvilammi 2020). Such thinking could be enriched by considering time and scale as we have done in this chapter. That is, the achievement of synergy across policies would need to go beyond the general orientation towards planetary boundaries and social floors and include concrete ideas at what scales (local, national, transnational) particular policies should be applied and in which temporal sequence.

Notes

1 The primacy ascribed to the local-level steering in much of the literature is related to the vision of a thoroughly localised economy. That is, localisation advocates highlight the need to replace the current global production and trade systems with economies based on cooperative principles and oriented towards local production and consumption cycles (Dietz and O'Neill 2013). Some local and voluntary grassroots initiatives have proven quite efficient in environmental terms even though they often face difficulties in sustaining themselves over time (Howell 2012). While some of the obstacles to local production cycles could be removed in the context of degrowth, it is still the case that much production cannot feasibly be made entirely local. For this reason alone, state activities at different scales would be desirable in degrowth transformations.

2 The alternative, currently favoured by most capitalist states, is to reach agreements with transnational corporations on 'voluntary' withdrawals from fossil fuel energy production. For instance, RWE, historically one of the top 100 individual greenhouse gas emitters, will receive over 2.8 billion euros in compensation from the German government for the exit from coal in 2030. However, in the meantime, RWE is allowed to expand and intensify the burning of fossil fuels; hence the struggle about the by-now famous village of Lützerath, below which lie an additional 280 Mio tonnes of CO_2 in the shape of lignite coal.

3 For an analysis of the Paris Agreement, see e.g., Morgan (2016).

4 Though countries with coordinated forms of capitalism have not yet achieved better ecological results than uncoordinated ones, the governments of the countries with coordinated capitalism may nevertheless be in a better position to initiate a degrowth transformation based on a deprioritisation of growth. In fact, recent comparative attitude studies (Fritz and Koch 2019; Otto and Gugushvili 2020) show that support rates for 'sustainable welfare' (see below) strategies are the highest by citizens of social-democratic countries.

5 While human needs theories can be traced back to Aristotle (Lamb and Steinberger 2017), the two most systematic and influential approaches have been (independently) tabled by Doyal and Gough (1991) and Max-Neef (1991) in the early 1990s. Doyal and Gough identified adequate nutritional food and water, adequate protective housing, non-hazardous work and physical

environments, appropriate healthcare, security in childhood, significant primary relationships, physical security, economic security, safe birth control and child-bearing, and basic education as 'general characteristics' to meet the two basic human needs of 'physical and mental health' and 'autonomy of agency'. Max-Neef (1991: 32–3) suggested subsistence, protection, affection, understanding, participation, idleness, creation, identity and freedom as universal needs, each of which can be expressed through needs satisfiers in the four dimensions of being, having, doing and interacting.

6 It would be interesting to study if, due to their dominated position within the state, employees located in what Bourdieu calls its 'left hand' (welfare and environmental state, for example) are more susceptible to such self-transformation than the currently dominating members of the judiciary and financing departments (located on the state's 'right hand').

6

Business in degrowth transformations

Having considered civil society and the state in degrowth transformations, we now turn to the role of business. In recent years, discussions in the degrowth literature have increasingly revolved around issues related to 'degrowth business' – or some other combination of the terms 'degrowth/post-growth' and 'business/organisation' (Hankammer et al. 2021; Nesterova 2020a, 2020b; Schmid 2018). Such discussions have sought to come to terms with what business would be like as part of a degrowth society, if it can indeed be part of it (Nesterova and Robra 2022), and what, if any, roles business can play in transformations towards such societies. In what follows, we first provide some general reflections on degrowth and business, explaining why we regard the latter to be an important actor on the roads to degrowth. As in the preceding chapters, we then consider various matters related to scale and diversity before we analyse what practices businesses would need to implement to render them consistent with degrowth. We end the chapter with a contemplation of whether a degrowth business is necessarily a non-growing business – concluding that this is not the case.

A primer on business and degrowth

Within the degrowth discourse, some claim that business in most of its forms is simply inconsistent with degrowth. The reasoning is that whereas the business is an inherently capitalist entity established to seek, make and maximise profit (Nesterova and Robra 2022), degrowth is both anti- and post-capitalist. Here, Perlman's logic is followed. Perlman notes that a 'businessman is a human being whose living humanity has been thoroughly excavated' (Perlman 1983: 31). Others assume that business can indeed be part of a degrowth society. Or they assume that at the very least business can be part of the journey towards such a society, whereas the final elements of a degrowth society remain obscure (Nesterova 2020a; Trainer 2012).

We agree with the second viewpoint for two reasons. First, businesses currently exist in large numbers. Thus, a strategy of some kind is necessary for them to participate in a broader societal transformation – in cooperation with social forms in civil society (Chapter 4) and the state (Chapter 5). To exclude the domain of business, a large part of the modern economy, from a theory of degrowth transformations seems unwise. Moreover, while some businesses are not compatible with degrowth, businesses operating in destructive sectors being cases in point, there are also forms of business which can be compatible with and part of a degrowth economy. Moreover, it seems likely that a time will come when uncomfortable questions such as 'how about multinational corporations?' will need to be asked in relation to degrowth and answered in more sophisticated ways than proposing that they will not exist in a degrowth society.

Our second reason for viewing business as part of degrowth is the acknowledgement that human beings are central to business. Individuals who are currently owner-managers and employees of businesses may not be opposed to transformations, and in fact be supportive of both sustainability more broadly and even degrowth as a strand of sustainability thinking if they (come to) know what it is. Some people may be participating in business due to the absence – or their unawareness – of other choices rather than because they aim to reproduce the capitalist system and maximise profits by exploiting fellow humans, non-humans and nature. Ironically, claiming that a business is necessarily a profit-maximising entity is relying on the same logic as neoclassical economics, the school of thought from which degrowth tries to deviate and whose premises it counters.

Making a distinction between business as trade and a business as a social entity (for example, a company or firm) can be helpful. If degrowth society is seen as a journey rather than as something that can be brought into existence overnight (Nesterova 2022c), it is to be expected that *trade* would remain part of degrowth society, even if such a society were in later stages to move towards consumers becoming producers, greater self-sufficiency, low technology, and even barter (Skrbina and Kordie 2021). Yet what are some of the transformations that business as trade could undergo on journeys towards degrowth society? For one thing, business as global trade would need to be reduced, since long supply chains are unsustainable, energetically and materially intensive, and obscure. More human needs should be satisfied locally and in a place-sensitive manner, where the meaning of 'location' can be fluid rather than precisely defined (for example, as a town) depending on a product or service. More alternative forms of business and organisations would participate in trade (Nesterova and Robra 2022). Moreover, fewer activities would in general be carried out by 'doing business'. This includes less marketisation and less commercialisation. Indeed, in a degrowth society more space (physical and metaphorical) should be dedicated to other activities outside business, and opportunities should be sought which allow people to produce goods themselves (in households) and collectively via, for example, community-based organisations (Trainer 2012). In other words, in a degrowth society not only production and consumption would be reduced, so would exchange or trade. Instead, other forms of redistribution of both goods and skills can be employed, such as sharing, gift and provision (for example, via universal basic services).

Turning to businesses as *social entities*, 'degrowth business' is a term that has so far mostly been used to refer to a business suitable for a degrowth society.[1] What would business look like in such a society and during transformations towards it? A business can engage in transformations in at least two ways. First, it can be self-transformed via the intentional efforts of humans involved in the business, such as businesspersons and even employees, naturally considering the difference in power of those groups as well as the policy environment in which the business exists. Second, it can be transformative towards social structures it is embedded in, possibly by collaborating with actors in civil society and the state. These processes are deeply interrelated. In transforming itself, a business also contributes to transforming socio-economic structures (Nesterova 2021c), and business-as-usual becomes less acceptable and less desirable. For instance, nurturing a fellow-feeling by owner-managers and employees towards nature goes against the current norm of exploitation and seeing nature as merely a resource pool. Such attitudes may find manifestations in the practices of the business in which these people are involved. Transforming the business itself may encourage its networks as well as customers to reconsider their own relationships with nature, prompting them, for instance, to make more ecological choices and source more sustainable materials. While this may appear almost unrealistic and a utopian view of business, our own work with businesspersons shows that often they are normal human beings who are not any less concerned with the state of the world around them than are other people (e.g., Nesterova 2020b, 2022c). It is often the case that businesspersons do not promote or support degrowth because they do not know about it or were educated or brought up believing that capitalism is the only system that works.

Theoretically, business can be seen as both an agent in economies and societies, as well as a structure. Viewing business as a structure places focus on the transformation of business via the agency of the individuals involved in business. In this case, the interest is in internal processes, relationships, hierarchies, power, culture, teams and dynamics. Disambiguating a business as a structure and considering its internal principles and logics allows one to appreciate the depth of transformation, which goes all the way to the psyches of the individuals involved. Viewing business as an agent focuses on the role of business as a single social entity and how this entity can participate in transforming the social world as an agent. In this case, the relationships between businesses, the empowering and constraining structures a business is subject to, are the aspects to consider. Neither focus suffices on its own, and both remain important. For instance, it is challenging to imagine that a business can become an agent of change if it is not also transformed as a structure.

Scales and diversity of business in degrowth transformations

In this section we consider various matters related to the scale and diversity of degrowth business. The first thing to note here is that business comes in different scales, ranging from micro businesses and sole traders (sole proprietorship), in which case the businessperson is also the business entity, to large transnational corporations which themselves represent complex structures and systems of ownership and subsidiaries spread across numerous locations. With degrowth advocating reduced matter and energy throughput, qualitative change, localisation, production for needs and redistribution of power, it is safe to assume that transnational corporations will not form part of degrowth societies. The reason for this is that such corporations are characterised by, for instance, obscure ownership patterns, enormous power, including the power to shape and direct consumption, and highly unequal remuneration of workers. The most suitable scales of business for degrowth are the micro and small scales. Some argue, however, that large-scale production and service provision such as steelworks and railways would continue to exist in a degrowth society (Trainer 2012). This is indeed likely, unless a degrowth society is understood to be a highly localised, low-technology society (see e.g., Skrbina and Kordie 2021). If such a society does not seem realistic or even desirable, then degrowth theorists need to contemplate challenging questions such as what will happen with large-scale production and transnational corporations on the journey towards a degrowth society. Moreover, if industries such as the railways industry and steelworks are deemed desirable, many more industries become necessary. That is, like any other industries, the railways and steel industries do not exist in a vacuum: they require supply chains, complex machinery and equipment which, in turn, require large and high-technology factories.

While it may be controversial to see large-scale producers as allies of degrowth, to exclude them entirely from discussions of transformations is unwise. Interestingly, degrowth scholars often advocate services provided and made possible by large corporations (such as travelling by train), while also seeing such companies as not immediately degrowth compatible. Arguably, other strands of sustainability thinking such as circular economy and green capitalism scholarship – including various corporate social responsibility discourses – have been more attentive to the sustainability question of large-scale production and have not shied away from contemplating the role of large corporations in bringing about a sustainable society and proposing ideas for their participation (for example, business models, certification). While we do not consider large corporations the ideal form of degrowth business (or even suitable for degrowth society), focusing mostly on small firms or alternative organisations and theorising ideal degrowth organisations does not suffice.

How can large businesses become more degrowth compatible? First and foremost, the question of (fair and more transparent) ownership may be reflected upon. In contemporary capitalism it is typically incredibly challenging to understand the structure of a large company's ownership, especially because it is common for companies to own and control other companies as is the case with holding companies. Statements such as the following from Fair Squared GmbH (2022) are rare: 'FAIR SQUARED is a limited company registered in Cologne, Germany. The company is family owned with no other companies or investors directly or indirectly involved. Our headquarters and warehouse are located on 700 m² rented space in Cologne Marsdorf. Additional warehouse capacity is available through logistics providers if and when needed.' Complicated ownership structures exist for the purpose of valorisation of capital rather than for the purpose of production for genuine human needs in a society living in harmony with nature. It remains unclear whether an appropriate path for degrowth is to pursue nationalisation (public ownership) beyond selected industries. Such a path may lead to bureaucratic structures and require a strong state able to manage vast resources (see also Chapter 5). A mixture of ownership can also be pursued, for instance, if only large-scale production and service provision is run by the state (such as railways or steelworks) while the majority of other types of production and service provision is owned by communities or individuals.

Micro and small-scale businesses are more degrowth compatible for several reasons. Such businesses do not possess the same level of power as transnational corporations and many such businesses are localised in various ways such as with respect to ownership, operation, employment or sourcing. Localisation is an important aspect of degrowth society (Latouche 2009; Trainer 2014). However, localisation of ownership and operation is distinct from localisation of supply chains. For instance, even a simple bar of soap produced in Sweden requires materials from far-away destinations: shea butter from Ghana and essential oil from France. Producing wine from local wild berries in Northern Sweden (based on an example from our own research) requires equipment imported from Italy, expertise from Canada and laboratory services from Denmark. Thus, often the 'local' appearance of a company conceals what actually goes into the production of a certain product.

Small-scale business can lead to positive outcomes for humans (and nature). For instance, small businesses can ensure a higher level of control over the processes of production and responsibility towards a place. They can also create spaces for psychological wellbeing (Nesterova 2022b). Such outcomes are due to a small business's ownership patterns, embeddedness within their local community and their independence. However, scale does not in itself qualify a business for a degrowth society. Even a small business can be hierarchical and a less than pleasant space to work in. Such businesses might also not have dedicated human resources departments which could assist in, for instance, conflict resolution. Smallness of business also does not guarantee better practices. A small business can focus on niche products which are unaffordable for the general public, or common products which are likewise unaffordable precisely due to the small and local nature of a business. For instance, Russell (1994) mentions innumerable unnecessary small shops in London that operated for the leisure of the idle rich. While Russell's example goes back over 80 years, his critique remains as relevant today. Businesses in a degrowth economy should focus on the satisfaction of genuine human needs and do so in a manner which allows more people to consume the product. In other words, it is important to contemplate each business individually rather than rely on broad statements such as 'small is beautiful' (Schumacher 1993). It may or may not be – or it may be for some but not for others.

In a degrowth society, businesses would be likely to assume a diversity of legal *forms*. They could, for instance, take the form of private companies, cooperatives, not-for-profit businesses or (eco-) social enterprises. Crucially, the form of business, just like the scale of business, in itself does not determine its degrowth compatibility. In other words, a degrowth society would not be brought about if all existing privately held companies (of various legal forms such as 'limited' in the UK and 'GmbH' in Germany) suddenly became cooperatives. A small privately held company can be a pleasant place to work in, it can be non-growing and practise ecological orientation and pro-sociality. A cooperative can be hierarchical, have unhealthy internal dynamics and produce products which are unnecessary.

The best approach to organising production and service provision in a degrowth society would probably be to allow for a plurality of organisational forms and ways of cooperation. Each form has its positive aspects and downsides. For instance, private companies can offer a person or a group of people more control over the company's operations. This might be the most suitable form for, say, a small-scale artisanal and craft production firm (Nørgård 2013), as well as for small local cafés and stores. Such firms can still cooperate with others, for example by sharing resources and collectively implementing circular economy practices, fulfilling larger-scale projects in cooperation and establishing formal and informal networks (Nesterova and Buch-Hansen 2023; see also Savini 2023). Such firms may allow individuality and relative autonomy – and facilitate a higher level of wellbeing for those who prefer to operate a small business by themselves or in cooperation with friends and family. Doing so is not necessarily a sign of individualism or egocentrism and does not go against the principles of a degrowth society.

Larger-scale production of food, for example, can be organised in a degrowth society in the form of a cooperative and, for instance, be owned by workers. Again, however, this is not the only degrowth-compatible form such production can take. Food production can likewise be carried out by small-scale independent farmers. In the degrowth discourse, some have placed hope in cooperatives as a prevalent form of business in a degrowth society (see e.g., Johanisova et al. 2015). However, while such a form can be beneficial since it emphasises counter-capitalist values such as democratic member control, it may not be the most suitable form for some strands within anarchist tradition (Stirner 2005). For instance, some may see a democratic structure as constraining, and membership in a cooperative as an obligation or a pressure to participate. Such an individualist perspective is not necessarily incompatible with degrowth if one assumes human goodness to be central to human nature (see Conclusion, this volume).

Apart from cooperatives, (eco-) social enterprises have been proposed as a form of business for a degrowth society (Johanisova and Franková 2017). Such businesses, as the name suggests, prioritise ecological and social outcomes over profits. In doing so, they reinvest profits into ecological and social commitments and projects. The distinction between such forms and a 'normal' business is not always clear. While it may be assumed that a 'normal' business prioritises profits and ignores ecological and social embeddedness, it is not necessarily so in reality. Especially in the case of small companies, what practices and principles are prioritised depends on the owner-managers as well as the employees of the business (Nesterova 2021a). Some business owners operate their business less with a view to pursue profit and more for cultural reasons, as a family tradition and/or as a commitment to a certain location. In other words, a business can behave akin to an (eco-) social enterprise without necessarily being one or identifying itself as such.

Above we have considered some of the diverse forms that businesses can take in degrowth transformations. However, if society were to embark and progress on degrowth journeys, it is conceivable that the differences between these diverse forms of business eventually become less prominent. That is, ultimately, the need for a specific form such as 'not-for-profit business', '(eco-) social enterprise', 'community interest company' etc. may become obsolete in a degrowth society where all businesses would deviate from the primacy of profit seeking and find more freedom to pursue other commitments, many of which businesses are pursuing already.

Degrowth business practices

In this section, we contemplate what practices businesses could implement to become degrowth compatible. To this end we use the four planes of social being model (Bhaskar 2020: 116; Bhaskar 1993) outlined in the book's Introduction so as to provide a holistic perspective. We suggest that business transformations would pertain to their transactions with nature, relationships between people, social structure and people's selves (Table 1). For this reason, elsewhere we identify degrowth business as a business of deep transformations (Nesterova 2022b). Certainly, it is not always straightforward to assign specific business practices to a specific plane. For instance, localisation of production can be seen as a degrowth practice of improving humanity's material transactions with nature. Yet it can also facilitate a closer connection between the business and the people in the location in which the business is. Likewise, moral growth, a kind of growth that should be welcomed and nurtured in a degrowth society, may naturally result in rethinking of business's relationship with nature and its practices in this domain. In other words, the planes are interconnected, a matter we return to in the Conclusion to the volume.

Starting with *material transactions with nature*, an overall goal of a degrowth economy is the reduction in humanity's matter and energy throughput. This does not necessarily easily translate to the level of business. Still, businesses can contribute to this pursuit by centring their production around the principle of sufficiency, that is, produce what is needed and not more. A firm may also be able to decrease the wastes that go into the environment. This can be achieved, for instance, by revising the process of production and by working with other businesses that can make use of the wastes created by a firm. For instance, cardboard waste generated by one firm may be shredded and used by another firm to package its products (Nesterova 2020b). Here, degrowth business can in both practice and theory benefit from existing knowledge of how to close matter and energy

Table 1 Degrowth business practices and the four planes of social being

Planes of social being	Practices
Material transactions with nature	Sufficiency in energy and material use Waste and pollution minimisation Efficiency in the use of materials/energy, circularity Renewable resource/energy use Durable and repairable products Localisation of production
Social interactions between people	Non-hierarchy Democratic decision-making Wellbeing Work as a process of learning and growth Knowledge sharing Collaboration
Social structure	Appropriate technology Decreased productivity Reduction in working hours Embeddedness within society Production for needs satisfaction Plurality of business forms Working with likeminded businesses, activists and consumers Transparent and fair ownership patterns
Inner being	Moral growth Non-anthropocentrism Long-term view Fellow-feeling towards humans and non-humans

Source: Adapted from Nesterova (2020a, 2021a).

loops in the process of production by implementing circularity as a principle (Bauwens 2021; Nesterova and Buch-Hansen 2023).

Using renewable material and energy is a degrowth business practice. However, it is doubtful whether renewable energy can sustain a degrowth society (Trainer 2022), especially considering the aspirational and theoretical nature of a degrowth society. That is, it remains unclear what such a society will look like and what will be produced in it, how it will be produced and by whom. In this case, renewable energy use needs to be combined with other practices, such as sufficient and efficient production. Another important practice is producing goods which are durable and repairable.

This means deviating from single-use products and packaging (including near-single-use products such as fast fashion and fast furniture), planned obsolescence and other common but destructive practices. Production of durable and repairable items can support the efforts of degrowth-compatible social movements. As described in Chapter 4, such movements may include the zero-waste movement as well as minimalism and voluntary simplicity. Consumers who align themselves with such movements seek to engage in slower and more mindful consumption and demand durable and repairable products. In a degrowth society such movements would probably become the norm.

As mentioned above, yet another important aspect of degrowth business practice is localisation (Nesterova 2022b; Trainer 2012). Localisation is not only or simply about the shortening of supply chains, thereby improving humanity's material transactions with nature. It is also about practising responsibility towards places and embeddedness within them. This may include understanding the local culture, knowing one's community, understanding the rhythms of local nature and climate, the patterns of topography and the patterns of the social life. Clarke (2013: 496) notes that 'localities are not produced and then fixed in perpetuity, but get made, unmade and remade over time'. Businesses can participate in this process of making or transforming localities towards more ecological ones, rendering them better places to dwell in for humans and non-humans alike.

Turning to *social interactions between people*, they would undergo a significant transformation in degrowth business. Non-hierarchical organisation can enable democratic decision-making where everyone can participate in the process of business transformation. Interactions between businesspeople should be aimed at wellbeing, learning and fulfilment in the process of production rather than competition. Replacing competition with cooperation and collaboration could likewise facilitate knowledge sharing and mentoring of fellow workers. Improved social interactions between business and the surrounding community can materialise if a business considers not only the location where it is, but also the place. The notion of a place goes far beyond that of a location (Tuan 1979, 2001) in that a place is defined as a 'particular location that has acquired a set of meanings and attachments' (Cresswell 2009: 169). Business, alongside its customers and participants in networks, can develop a shared meaning, for instance, exemplified in a collective desire for harmonious coexistence. Also, it can arrange economic interactions in ways making co-existence possible. This requires expanding the notion of social interactions beyond the ones internal to business to also include the interactions between the business and its 'outside'.

Next, we contrast existing *social structures* with what could be transformative structures both within and outside business. Usually, social structures are seen as constraining towards degrowth business. This is indeed so if the social system is seen as uniformly capitalist and homogeneous. However, within contemporary societies and economies, a diversity of structures and practices exists (Chapter 2; see also Gibson-Graham and Dombroski 2020). Some social structures can be empowering towards degrowth businesses. Such structures include formal and informal networks as well as the presence of like-minded businesses and customers (or even activists and politicians) who share similar worldviews and are likewise on a journey towards a society living in harmony with nature. Business as a social structure can be organised in a variety of forms. As we discussed above, no form is perfect, and the plurality of forms should be highlighted. No matter which forms a degrowth business assumes, its ownership patterns should be fair and transparent.

While many businesses exist as abstract and mobile entities in the capitalist system, a degrowth business is embedded within other social structures in its location. Such embeddedness may be multi-scalar and refer to the business's own location, the broader region and nature at large. Embeddedness of a business is unavoidable. Production and service provision by degrowth businesses should be carried out for the purpose of satisfaction of genuine needs. Degrowth does not suggest that only basic needs must be satisfied, although satisfaction of basic human needs of all humans sufficiently is non-negotiable and should become a priority.

While indeed there is much that businesses can do by themselves, for example by organising networks or working with suppliers and distributors with similar worldviews, a range of *policies* could also assist business participation in the transformation of societal structures. Policies can target various levels of business. Universal basic income can facilitate the creation of small businesses engaged in artisanal and craft production. It can offer humans some 'breathing space' to deviate from their current, often meaningless, employment (Graeber 2018) and do something in which they find meaning and fulfilment, for example, turn their existing hobby into a small business. The costs, both in terms of identity and income, of quitting a job and establishing a degrowth-inspired business instead, are rather high. In the capitalist system, the risk is likewise high. A basic income and the provision of universal basic services can counter some of this risk.

Currently, policies facilitate conventional, capitalist dynamics. For instance, they aim to support growing businesses which comply with the capitalist definition of success and that can demonstrate growth aspirations. Support should be given to a much wider range of businesses, including those businesses which operate in desirable sectors (such as organic agriculture) and those which do not seek to grow. Below we argue that a degrowth business is not necessarily a non-growing one, yet non-growing businesses should receive more recognition. In the capitalist setting, businesses often seek growth not due to a certain desire to sustain capitalism, but rather to address the issue of borrowing and debt. This dynamic is externally imposed. Addressing interest repayment can be a way of facilitating businesses that are more degrowth compatible. Policies in the current system likewise target technological innovation and digitalisation. Some argue that in a degrowth society the focus would be on appropriate and even simplified technology rather than high technology (Heikkurinen 2018; Heikkurinen and Ruuska 2021; Nesterova 2021b). Further to this, policies can provide support for businesses which make use of lower technology. Having said that, no consensus exists as regards the relationship between technology and degrowth. It may be that some technological innovations can serve degrowth transformations, for example by facilitating a more effective sharing of existing resources, items and food, gifting, borrowing and lending existing goods, organising for degrowth, learning about degrowth and sharing experiences.

Finally, degrowth business transformations would also pertain to the plane of *inner being*. This plane has so far not received much attention in the field of degrowth (Brossmann and Islar 2020; Buch-Hansen and Nesterova 2023). A reason for this may be that degrowth scholarship seeks to deviate from methodological individualism, that is, explaining what happens in society with reference to the actions of individual humans. The degrowth discourse often emphasises social structures and systems and humanity's material transactions with nature, thus tending to overlook people's inner life. Degrowth advocates tend to suggest that to transition towards a degrowth society, humans need to organise with others, collaborate and cooperate. While we have no argument with this, it is also important to recognise that there are differences between individuals. For this reason, it is important that degrowth business is diverse and allows different people to choose different forms of business, production and provision which can be more or less collective, ranging from being self-sufficient to relying on networks and communities.

We would contend that growth in people's inner being is universally required for transformations towards degrowth to become reality. This applies equally to businesspersons and employees of businesses. Such growth may signify a shift towards harmonious coexistence between humans and nature, and hence make the degrowth business practices outlined above appealing to businesspersons and employees. Orientation towards harmonious coexistence is in stark contrast with what the current capitalist system promotes: short-term goals, overproduction and overconsumption, monetary gains, power and status seeking, and materialism. Implementation of degrowth business practices, which often go against the norms of the capitalist system, is a daunting process. However, growth in people's inner being would make this process meaningful and valuable. Such growth is a journey. Undoubtedly, as indicated above, business transformation should be seen in a similar way.

It is disempowering and unnecessarily pessimistic to assume that currently businesses are not doing anything to contribute to making degrowth society reality and that profit maximisation is the only pursuit businesspersons have. Typically, degrowth is not explicitly considered by businesses, but multiple practices that businesses currently engage in and multiple principles according to which they operate are degrowth compatible. An absence of the word 'degrowth' or a lack of knowledge about this concept does not mean that something akin to degrowth is not unfolding in the pockets and niches of the capitalist system and in the ways agents relate to the world, including within businesses.

It is important to remember that businesses are communities of humans. While the degrowth discourse revises every premise of mainstream economics and assumes that 'economic man' is a false and misleading model of a human being (see Chapter 4), it at the same time assumes that those involved in business, especially owner-managers, are 'economic men' working intentionally towards the reproduction of capitalist structures. Empirical work reveals that this is not the case, even if it may be the case in some businesses (e.g., Nesterova 2021a). Individuals are different and they employ a great diversity of practices in their businesses. Like other humans, owner-managers and employees are in their own ways trying to navigate the capitalist landscape and have varying views in terms of personal practice, politics, and how they relate with others, nature and non-humans. In their capacity as consumers, hardly any degrowth scholars are able to practise degrowth fully and live according to the principles we advocate (see also Ehrnström-Fuentes and Biese 2022). It is likewise unfair to expect that businesses can be fully degrowth compatible in the capitalist system.

In conclusion: growth vs non-growth

In the early development of the degrowth discourse, it was common to translate the goal of an overall reduction in matter and energy throughput into the notion that non-growth is necessary at the level of business. The relationship between humanity's reduction in matter and energy throughput and the so-called microeconomic level is, however, much less straightforward. Moving towards an economic system that functions within planetary boundaries does not mean that no businesses can grow or indeed that consumption cannot increase in some cases. In other words, a degrowth business is not necessarily a business which does not grow (although it can also be a non-growing business). Imposing non-growth on businesses, especially micro and small business, is oversimplifying and mathematising the issue – something that was common in earlier growth-critical scholarship (see e.g., Daly and Townsend 1993). It is more fruitful to pay attention to the quality, nature and journey of a business as a community of individuals who are trying to navigate the capitalist landscape, hopefully towards a better world. Moreover, mathematising the issue and prescribing, for instance, how many items a business can produce or how many employees it can have, requires bureaucratic oversight and top-down control. The questions then arise of who would be overseeing and enforcing such rules or guidelines, how much power they would have and whether a market would be created for trading various permits for quantities. A change in values and culture, whereby individuals internalise non-capitalist pursuits, appears to be a more sustainable option in relation to a long-term change.

As we noted in the book's Introduction, growth in some parts of a degrowth economy is in fact desirable and necessary. For instance, growth in the number and size of businesses involved in organic agriculture does not contradict degrowth. Craft and artisanal production is also often highlighted positively in the degrowth discourse (Nørgård 2013; Soper 2020). It may thus be expected that the number of such businesses would grow, and that existing businesses of this sort could expand their production and employ several more people. New possibilities in the built environment open spaces for alternative buildings and modes of living, thus new businesses may be established in this industry, just as existing ones may grow (Nesterova 2022a). This does not mean that no limits should be placed on business. For example, allowing businesses to turn into transnational corporations is counterproductive for a degrowth economy.

Overall, a more holistic approach to business growth needs to be taken. The scientific community as well as practitioners may consider deviating from the growth vs non-growth binary and see the question of growth in more processual terms. For instance, a business may grow in some periods of time when a new and good idea arises but maintain its capacity in other periods of time. Other businesses may not want to grow (Nesterova 2020b). Some businesses face increasing demand which they cannot satisfy since satisfaction of this demand comes at a cost of reduced quality of life. Still others may want to remain a certain size but are forced to expand to meet their debt obligations. A degrowth economy should offer more space for creativity and imagination as well as flexibility in engaging in business ventures. As consumers also transform their ways of relating with the world towards harmonious co-existence and thus consuming less, some businesses may naturally reduce their product ranges and even shrink. For such an attitude towards business growth to become reality, culture needs to change. Currently business growth is seen in hierarchical terms, as necessarily better than non-growth or more creative growth, or growth to a certain limit. Business growth is seen as a manifestation of success and entrepreneurial abilities. Transformations towards a degrowth economy require that such logics are challenged and deconstructed. This has major implications for business education including that in business schools and economics departments as well as in other fields of knowledge which derive from economics and business (such as economic geography).

Note

1 By a business we mean a social entity which produces and provides services. While recently a number of scholars have taken an interest in degrowth organisations (e.g., Vandeventer and Lloveras 2021), we avoid the use of the term 'organisation' in this context due to this term being even broader. That is, an organisation can encompass such greatly diverse social forms as, for example, religious organisations, informal organisations or institutions. A business can be seen as an organisation of production and service provision, and some organisations are engaged in business practices, community-supported agriculture being an example.

7

Degrowth transformations – an empirical study

Though the main contribution of this book is theoretical, it is important to indicate how our approach may inspire empirical studies into degrowth transformations. Much theorising would indeed be in vain if it could not illuminate the gap between theory and practice, which is especially obvious in the case of the climate emergency. For decades, scientists have predicted climate disaster, without this provoking much change in dominant production and consumption patterns or social practices. Social scientists are well positioned to shed light on this inertia of social structures, which, despite all their connections to the natural system, are different from natural structures. Worse still, remaining on the theoretical terrain risks reproducing what Bourdieu (2000: 51) called the 'scholastic fallacy': projecting one's 'theoretical thinking into the heads of acting agents', theorists have too often mixed up the world as an 'object of contemplation, a representation, a spectacle' with the world as it 'presents itself to those who do not have the leisure (or the desire) to withdraw from it in order to think it'.[1] In a political and strategic perspective, too, an empirical investigation into the type and share of people susceptible and opposed to degrowth transformations may be an important contribution to such change.

Previous chapters have identified eco-social policies as a key mechanism for degrowth transformations. Thus, in this chapter, a part of the book's theoretical perspective is applied in an analysis of the support for such policies. Specifically, we reinterpret recent quantitative and qualitative data from research projects in which Max Koch was involved in Sweden and relate these data to the four planes of social being. We start with a description of the support in the Swedish population[2] towards selected eco-social policies that degrowth and sustainable welfare scholars identified as important mechanisms of transformational change (see Hirvilammi et al. 2023 for an overview). This is followed by a more in-depth view into the kind of social groups in favour of and opposed to degrowth transformations. Finally, we introduce a method that we regard as helpful for the expansion of alternative societal spaces and thus the support for degrowth. We show

how the codified knowledge of researchers can be combined with the practical knowledge of citizens in the perspective of initiating transformative change, and present corresponding qualitative data from deliberative citizen forums on needs satisfaction.

How popular are transformational eco-social policies?

To assess the popularity of key eco-social policies, the present chapter presents and interprets representative survey data from the projects Sustainable Welfare for a New Generation of Social Policy collected in 2021[3] and The New Urban Challenge: Models of Sustainable Welfare in Swedish Metropolitan Cities (2020).[4] Six policy items in Table 2 operationalise the policies regulating maximum levels of needs satisfaction. These are designed to respect the 'ceilings' or ecological boundaries of the 'safe and just operating space' (Chapter 5; Gough 2020; Khan et al. 2022). They include limiting living space per person, limiting the number of flights per person per year, introducing a cap on incomes from work and wealth ('maximum income'), a tax on wealth and meat consumption, and working time reduction. Five further items operationalise critical minimum levels or sufficiency 'floors' of needs satisfaction. These include an unconditional basic income (UBI) and the introduction or expansion of universal basic services (UBS) in the areas of water, public transport, electricity and internet provision.

Most of the policies designed to limit production and consumption patterns are rather unpopular. Over 70% are against limitations of living space and almost 60% are against limiting the number of flights a citizen can take during a year. Over half of the sample is against a tax on meat and a cap on incomes.[5] The somewhat less radical alternative of a wealth tax is, however, quite popular at 42.5%, and about the same percentage against. This policy was previously in place and is apparently still part of the Swedish collective memory. The most popular of the policy items regulating maximum levels of needs satisfaction is the reduction of working time. This policy enjoys support from over half of the population, whereas about a third is against it.

The selected policy items regulating critical minimum levels of needs satisfaction via the provision of universal basic services at low fees are very popular. About 50% are in favour of basic provision of water, 48% of electricity, 45% of internet and 54% of local public transportation. By contrast, the introduction of a universal basic income is by far the least popular policy suggestion, with over 70% against it. This should be seen together with the rather high approval rates for the different universal basic services proposals, indicating path dependency in a country with a tradition of universal services within a social-democratic welfare regime, especially in the health

Table 2 Support for eco-social policy proposals in Sweden (%)

	Policy items regulating maximum levels of needs satisfaction						Policy items regulating critical minimum levels of needs satisfaction				
	Limit living space (2021)	Limit number of flights (2021)	Limit (maximum) income (2021)	Tax on wealth (2020)	Tax on meat consumption (2020)	Working time reduction (2020)	UBI: Basic income (2020)	UBS: Water low fee (2021)	UBS: Public transport in nascent area low fee (2021)	UBS: Electricity low fee (2021)	UBS: Internet low fee (2021)
Against	70.4	59.7	50.7	42.7	52.7	31.4	71.1	25.1	22.6	25.9	24.6
Undecided	21.1	18.8	22.1	14.8	17.1	17.0	17.6	24.7	22.7	25.4	29.0
In favour	8.4	21.4	27.2	42.5	30.3	51.6	11.3	50.2	54.7	48.8	46.5

Sources: Representative surveys conducted within the projects The New Urban Challenge: Models of Sustainable Welfare in Swedish Metropolitan Cities (2020) and Sustainable Welfare for a New Generation of Social Policy (2021). Respondents were asked to evaluate the above policy suggestions and answered on five-point Likert scales that contained the following categories: very good and fairly good ('in favour'), quite bad and very bad ('against'), neither good nor bad ('undecided').

and care sectors. Further contributing factors include the rather articulated work ethic in Sweden, according to which full-time employment is expected for men and women. It seems indeed easier to expand universal basic services in these institutional circumstances than to implement a universal basic income system with unclear consequences for service provision. However, in countries with a liberal welfare tradition and correspondingly rudimentary universal welfare provision, universal basic incomes may well be the quickest and easiest way forward to safeguard basic needs satisfaction (see Koch 2022b and Khan et al. 2022 for more detailed discussions).

Taken together, the survey results point to a considerable gap between most of the far-reaching measures that sustainability researchers consider necessary to address the climate emergency and the measures that Swedish citizens presently support.[6] However, approval rates for guaranteeing minimum needs satisfaction levels – universal basic services schemes in particular – are much higher than for measures oriented at introducing maximum levels. Explanation for the hesitation to implement policies targeting maximum levels of needs satisfaction may include normalisation and naturalisation of the growth imperative in people's minds and day-to-day social practices (Koch 2018a). As a corollary, the 'trickle-down effect', celebrated by neoliberal economists, according to which policymakers should not target the revenues of the rich because some of their gains will automatically benefit the greater good, is deeply anchored in the consciousness of many people. Welfare systems and multiple other institutions (legal, educational) historically co-developed with the provision of economic growth and remain coupled to it. The existence of this link is engrained in collective consciousness, as a result of which any political move beyond the capitalist growth economy needs to reckon with concerns about wellbeing loss and social exclusion (Büchs and Koch 2017).

However, not all people are equally disposed to the normalisation of the capitalist growth imperative. In what follows, we provide an analysis of how attitudes on eco-social policies and transformational change are linked to the four planes of transactions with nature, social interactions, social structures and inner being.

Eco-social dispositions and habitus types

Sociological understandings of the relationship of inertia and change are linked to positionings in the 'structure–agency' debate. The challenge is to explain how societal structures result as intended and often unintended consequences of individual practices. Different sociologists have emphasised either 'objective' structures or 'subjective' action, or positioned themselves at different points in a corresponding structure–action continuum (Koch 2020a). At one extreme of this continuum are positions which examine the whole of society and its institutions as interrelated systems first and then make their way down to address individuals and small-scale interactions.[7] At the opposite end of the spectrum are interactionist approaches that work their way up from the analysis of individual intentions and small-scale relationships to institutions and entire societies.[8]

We are drawn to intermediate positions in the structure–agency debate, represented for example by Marx, Bourdieu, critical realism and 'social practice' approaches (Røpke 2009; Shove et al. 2012; Bhaskar 2016; Büchs and Koch 2017). These take the position that social structures are – mostly unintended – results of individual actions. Bourdieu's theory of practice (understood as repeated, regular and routinised forms of individual action) simultaneously distances itself from structuralist (or objectivist) and interactionist (or subjectivist) positions (Bourdieu 1990). He introduces the habitus as a system of structured and structuring dispositions in terms of thoughts, perceptions, expressions and actions. Social agents are thought to be capable of making a difference, but always within the limits set by the historical period and the social conditions in which they live (Bourdieu 1993; Koch 2020a). This notion recognises that social structures are 'not literally internalized by individuals, but only metaphorically, through the influence they have on our subjectivity' (Elder-Vass 2007: 345). Following Bourdieu, it may be assumed that the dispositions of the habitus, acquired during socialisation in the family and the education system, are durable and for the most part subconscious. As such it constitutes an objective limitation to our capabilities and possibilities of creating societal alternatives. Yet human beings should also be considered reflexive and 'able to critically evaluate and thus modify our dispositions in the light of our experience, our reasoning capacities, and our value commitments' (Elder-Vass 2007: 345). The possibility of carrying out such reflexive choices is, however, unequally distributed in a structurally unequal society. In exploring the links between objective positions and subjective position-takings (Bourdieu 1998), we aim to understand why positive attitudes towards degrowth transformations are more likely within certain social contexts and groups than within others.[9] While the possibility of acting and initiating social change is generally limited by the socio-historical conditions of habitus formation, it also varies with one's position in society. People with more economic and cultural capital generally have greater impacts than others (Atkinson 2019: 954). Habitus types are combinations of 'traits' (Adorno et al. 1950) or 'dispositions' that are developed and occur in specific social contexts (Bremer and Teiwes-Kügler 2013: 161). It is essential not to schematically apply theoretically constructed habitus types but to generate them from the empirical material. Fritz et al. (2021) identify the dispositions and the habitus types in which they appear in the emerging Swedish eco-social field. The study also relates these dispositions to position-taking on various eco-social policies. In what follows, we refer to some of the study's main findings and reinterpret these in relation to people's susceptibility to degrowth transformations along the four planes of being.

Fritz et al. (2021) empirically identify eight dispositions that structure the eco-social field: state redistribution versus liberal market orientation, trust, self-transcendence versus self-enhancement, sustainable welfare, individualised environmentalism versus preference for traditional welfare policies ('red crowding-out'), neoliberal carelessness versus caring responsibility, 'fossilism', and power and control.[10] Differing significantly with respect to age, education, gender, income, occupation, religiosity, political orientation, climate and welfare policy preferences and practices such as flying or eating meat, seven clusters constituting typical combinations of these dispositions are identified below. We elaborate on the characterisation of the seven groups in Fritz et al. (2021) by commenting on their proximity and distance from degrowth transformations along the four planes.

The first habitus type, *passive anti-ecological conservativism*, is prevalent in about 10% of the sample, especially in the lower regions of social space and among older and retired persons. Among the employed respondents in this group, jobs with either a technical or an interpersonal work logic are frequent. Incomes are the lowest of all respondents, and education levels are lower than average. While men and women are about equally represented, religiosity is above average. Passive anti-ecological conservativism features anti-welfare attitudes and a more general 'neoliberal carelessness' (Fritz et al. 2021), which is reflected on all planes of social being, albeit in somewhat unique ways: in relation to transactions with nature, the view predominates that environmental protection should not be prioritised over economic growth. This is related to the perception of oneself as not being affected by climate change. Regarding social structure, benefits, services and social policies as means to address structural inequalities are rejected, and this is embedded in a more general scepticism towards the idea of a potentially positive role of the state in societal development. However, on the individual and social interaction planes, people with this habitus display the highest scores for 'self-transcendence' of an ecological kind, expressing concern and care for future generations as well as other human beings and species – a sort of care that takes an individualised and anti-collective form. Political 'position-takings' in terms of voting preferences reflect a deeply anchored reluctance towards societal change: the 'red-green' parties and the Liberals are rarely mentioned as preferred options, while the Sweden Democrats (a populist right-wing party) are overrepresented. The conservative trait of this habitus manifests itself in very high rejection rates of the statement that one's municipality should become 'more modern' 15 years from now. The 'passive' element – meaning a low involvement and interest in public affairs and civil society – is expressed by a low incidence of memberships in organisations and a reluctance to become active in improving welfare and the climate. For instance, three-quarters of this cluster ate meat and would not stop eating meat or flying, and would not join a demonstration.

The habitus trait of *self-centred privatism* is prevalent in about 8% of the sample, particularly among those with lower educational degrees and slightly below-average incomes. It is predominated by older persons, men, and skilled and unskilled workers. This group distinguishes itself by the highest scores for 'self-enhancement' (the opposite to 'self-transcendence'). That is, respondents are concerned with their personal and private matters and do not demonstrate much interest in broader political or societal issues, let alone transactions with nature, future generations or other human beings and species. Though this habitus type features a clear political tendency toward the right, with a preference for the Sweden Democrats, the Social Democrats are nevertheless also mentioned more often than average as preferred party. The evaluation of climate policies is a bit more negative than average, but not the worst among all clusters, while opinions about welfare policies do not differ much from the average. Similar to passive anti-ecological conservativism, the habitus of self-centred privatism involves a reluctance to become active in ecological and social matters. For example, over 70% would not stop eating meat or join a demonstration.

Environmental centralism is prevalent in a relatively large cluster (21% of the sample) and widespread among persons of average age, born in Sweden. It enjoys the uppermost socio-economic status due to typical work positions in the higher service class. Awareness of climate change is greater than average, indicating an acknowledgement that nature is a necessary precondition for any kind of social life. State action in this policy area is appreciated. Yet this is combined with laissez-faire views in relation to inequality and social structures more generally, whereby public welfare policies, particularly directed at economic inequality such as income tax and maximum and basic incomes, are rejected. There is also a liberal trait dominating perceptions of social interaction with others, expressed in moderate approval rates of an inclusive multiculturalism. In correspondence with the predominating upper locations in social space, people with this habitus feel immune when it comes to environmental risks and display low care for others. Yet in contrast to a plain market liberalism, environmental centralism is characterised by the highest trust for established institutions such as the government, political parties and trade unions. The unique combination of moderate and liberal habitus traits makes this cluster strategically central and contested. This is reflected in party preferences for the Centre and Liberal parties, which have in different political constellations joined the centre-left and centre-right blocs. While there is also some support for the Social Democrats and Greens, the political extremes (Left party and Sweden Democrats) are largely rejected. Concerning climate-related political practices, this cluster actively supports environment-friendly lifestyles, indicated by a greater than average approval of reduced meat consumption and flying.

The relatively large habitus group (16%) of *eco-modernist conservativism* assembles people of average education, income and socio-economic status. It consists of slightly older than average people, usually born in Sweden and living in rural areas. Sixty per cent are women. Employment in the lower service class is widespread, with over 40% having jobs with an interpersonal work logic. This corresponds to relatively high 'self-transcendence' scores: people in this group care for nature (also indicated by an advanced climate-change awareness and a rejection of fossil energy solutions), as well as other human beings and species. Yet, in relation to social structure, this is paired with a rather strong liberal market orientation and distrust in institutions, particularly the state. Inequality is, in other words, mostly seen as just and following from natural and meritocratic differences. Politically, this group is located on the right, with voting preferences for the Christian Democrats, Moderates and Sweden Democrats. The support for climate policies is average when it comes to personal contributions like increased taxes, but rather high concerning renewable energy and green electricity – measures that do not financially hurt directly and are compatible with 'ecological modernisation' and 'green growth', that is, market-driven ideas. Ideas about the 'autonomous individual' that should be left in peace by state and society in the interest of the common good are correspondingly popular and predominate imaginaries of the inner being.

The trait *fossil liberalism* is dominant in about 10% of the sample and typically found among male (over 70%) and urban people with higher incomes. Self-employment and independent and technical work predominate. The most distinctive disposition of this habitus type is what Fritz et al. (2021) call 'fossilism', the structural opposition to 'sustainable welfare', combining liberal market orientations, an animosity towards all kinds of climate and welfare policies, and a general lack of trust in institutions, particularly the state. Rejecting climate policies more than any other group, transactions with nature are interpreted in an almost exclusively instrumental way. Policies towards limiting inequalities within the social structure are likewise rejected. The individual's place in society and nature is regarded as justly deriving from one's own previous investments in work and educational system. One can conclude that 'others', human beings and species, are seen as mainly means to the end of individual achievement. Politically, this cluster holds views closest to the right, with party preferences split across the Christian Democrats, Moderates and Sweden Democrats.

About 19% of the sample feature the habitus of *active sustainable welfare*, in particular highly educated young people in urban areas, with an over-representation of women (57%) and non-religious persons (42%). With incomes somewhat below average and employment most often in interpersonal work contexts, and disposing of a maximum of cultural capital but merely average amounts of economic capital, this is the social group that is most receptive to degrowth transformations. It features high scores on 'self-transcendence', that is, environmental values indicating non-instrumental views on transactions with nature, and an advanced feeling of care responsibilities, be it towards other human beings or other species. The high regard of others and equality is also reflected in the imaginary of the social structure: the group displays the strongest support of egalitarian values and for welfare via state redistributive policies. As a corollary, the individual self is here typically perceived as embedded in the social and environmental context. Not surprisingly, this group tends to take political positions at the opposite pole from 'fossil liberalism' and 'passive anti-ecological conservativism', with clear preferences for the Greens and the Left Party. It features not only the strongest support for all kinds of climate and welfare policies but also the most frequent actual activities (from stopping flying and eating meat, demonstrating and social media posts, to lobbying politicians).

In contrast, the habitus type *moderate traditional welfare* includes persons with below average education and slightly below average incomes and socio-economic statuses (16% overall). It also features the highest share of persons not born in Sweden (25%) and of people who belong to some official religion (80%). Though welfare concerns are held in higher regard than environmental concerns, this group is largely in support of both (the exception being taxation of meat), featuring the highest scores for caring responsibility and slightly above average self-transcendence values. Hence, most people in this cluster neither prioritise economic growth over the environment nor present individual wants over future needs, indicating transformational potential both on the planes of material transactions with nature and inner being. Yet in relation to social structure, the support for welfare policies and state redistribution is average. Regarding interaction with others, this group submits to traditional hierarchical social relations and structures. Interestingly, people in this group hold individuals to be responsible for welfare and ecological degradation. It is politically drawn to the Social Democrats in combination with a dislike of Christian Democrats and the Left, taking positions somewhat left of the environmental centralists.

The seven habitus groups described and reinterpreted above in relation to their susceptibility to degrowth transformations are the empirical results of a relational approach in which political position-takings in the emerging eco-social field are assumed to be the products of the intersection of habitus, field and capital. What becomes apparent is the structural habitus traits that lie behind the attitudes towards policy suggestions that normally remain unconsidered and/or naturalised. Not only do the objective positions of the seven groups within society become intelligible, so do their relative distances, tensions and rupture lines, as well as their structural proximities and commonalities that complicate or facilitate the formation of political cross-group coalitions for and against degrowth transformations.

Understood in this relational way, the social structure displays somewhat contradictory features. On the one hand, climate change and related ecological threats have hitherto been picked up in rather classical and expected ways, the result being the reproduction rather than transformation of traditional social hierarchies (Fritz et al. 2021). The most 'progressive' social groups, featuring a maximum of cultural capital but finding themselves, in Bourdieu's terminology, at the 'dominated' end of the 'dominant' class, are at the forefront of degrowth and transformational change ('active sustainable welfare'). Meanwhile, the liberal right, characterised by a predominance of economic capital, is located at the opposite pole, resisting eco-social efforts ('fossil liberalism'). Not only do these two groups occupy opposite positions within the upper regions of social space and share correspondingly different dispositions and political position-takings (see Figure 2 in Fritz et al. 2021), they also differ fundamentally in relation to the four planes of social being, indicating different degrees of susceptibility to degrowth transformations (Table 3). In fact, these two groups are the only ones that display largely consistent habitus traits in their diametrically opposed perceptions of material transactions with nature, interactions with others, social structures and inner being. It is safe to say that a political convergence of the two structural poles can largely be excluded. Given the long-term inertia of habitus traits, people with the habitus of fossil liberalism are unlikely to be convinced by the degrowth movement anytime soon. Fortunately, this is a rather small group comprising about a tenth of the population.[11]

On the other hand, the vast majority of people today feature habitus structures of an inconsistent kind, displaying varying degrees of susceptibility to degrowth on different planes. This makes new coalitions for socio-ecological transformations at least conceivable. Fritz et al. (2021) consider the example of a political alliance between representatives of active sustainable welfare and environmental centralism. Such an alliance would not only be structurally possible, it would also be capable of mobilising sufficient symbolic and material capital to achieve cultural and political hegemony. Differences that would need to be overcome lie in the respective views on the roles of business and social justice in socio-ecological transformations.

Table 3 Degrowth transformational potentials of habitus groups along the planes of social being (O = Open to degrowth; S = Sceptical towards degrowth)

	Passive anti-ecological conservatism	Self-centred privatism	Environmental centralism	Eco-modernist conservativism	Fossil liberalism	Active sustainable welfare	Moderate traditional welfare
Material transactions with nature	S	S	O	O	S	O	O
Interaction with others	O	S	O	O	S	O	S
Social structures	S	O	O	S	S	O	S
Inner being	O	S	S	S	S	O	O

Moreover, they lie in the planes of inner being and interactions with others (see Table 3). Proponents of 'active sustainable welfare' envision individuals as embedded in wider natural and social webs in combination with exhibiting a feeling of care and responsibility towards them, while the liberal trait within 'environmental centralism' produces a tendency towards individualism and low levels of care. Nevertheless, on three of the four planes there is at least some degree of agreement between the two groups, which political activism could try to enhance.

Beyond the two just-mentioned habitus groups, people are not entirely against degrowth. To varying degrees on the different planes of social being they show some support for it. At this point it is worth remembering that habitus merely makes certain views and practices more likely than others. That is, it does not exclude the existence of other causal mechanisms behind practice, such as rational reasoning. The social sciences can generate knowledge that makes it possible to target specific habitus groups in different ways, considering their current positions and position-takings relative to the four planes of being. For example, when engaging with people characterised by habitus traits of 'moderate traditional welfare', one would need to think of ways to encourage them to contemplate their views on hierarchies and power. People in the habitus group of 'passive anti-ecological conservatism' could be encouraged to reflect on the way they view humanity's material transactions with nature. In the next section, we introduce a deliberative method of interaction between citizens, activists and researchers capable of facilitating such exchanges.

Deliberating degrowth transformations via citizen forums

Most people feature inconsistent habitus traits, making them more or less susceptible to degrowth transformations. This susceptibility may well increase in the current multidimensional crisis of capitalism. Yet whether the capitalist growth economy will eventually be overcome via a socio-ecological transformation and degrowth is far from certain. More often than not, the crisis of an established order has resulted in a new kind of orthodoxy where dominant interests are defended by replacing democratic rule by authoritarian rule and the use of force. New types of right-wing populist movements combine a conservative critique of finance-driven capitalism with chauvinistic and xenophobic slogans and provide the popular basis for an authoritarian solution to the crisis; that is, one in which the prevalent way of life in the rich countries is defended by, for instance, using military power and closing borders (Koch 2020a).

At this juncture, strategies for bottom-up mobilisations are critical. Such strategies also become possible due to a margin of freedom for political actions, projects and policies opening up at a time of crisis (Bourdieu 2000). These political actions and projects could rely on the dispositions of the habitus that are already susceptible to degrowth transformations, and be assisted by heterodox centres within academia. Academia can play a role in the processes of 'counter training' (Bourdieu 2000). This entails creation and expansion of spaces where the growth imperative ceases to occupy people's minds. Examples of existing spaces include degrowth conferences, associated local events, and larger-scale initiatives such as Transition towns (Chapter 4). An additional attempt of collaboration between researchers and other citizens are deliberative citizen forums, in which the knowledge of researchers, citizens and local stakeholders is combined to identify the goods and services necessary for sustainable needs satisfaction within a particular social context.

A framework for imagining and boosting transformational change is provided by the Human Scale Development methodology (Max-Neef 1991). It introduces a distinction between fundamental human needs, which are understood as largely universal across time and space, and needs satisfiers, which differ depending on specific historic, social and cultural contexts. Needs satisfiers may range from characteristics, attitudes, actions and norms to institutions, policies, physical environment or infrastructures and be operationalised at different scales and sites (including business, civil society and the state). Eleven citizen forums were carried out in 2020 on sustainable needs satisfaction in Sweden.[12] In total 84 individuals participated in discussions about how fundamental needs are satisfied today, and how this could be done in more sustainable ways. Forum participants discussed and distinguished between positive and negative needs satisfiers and then deliberated on linking satisfiers oriented at actions and measures to achieve an alternative future. In what follows, we relate selected forum data to our theoretical framework for degrowth transformations. Table 4 displays selected negative and Table 5 presents positive needs satisfiers as highlighted in the citizen forums in relation to the four planes of social being and the three sites of degrowth transformations: business, civil society and state. It is essential to recognise that any needs satisfier will exist simultaneously on all the four planes. Yet, it can also be argued that specific needs satisfiers feature more prominently on selected planes. Thus, in Tables 4 and 5 we assign specific needs satisfiers to one plane only to serve as examples.

In the site of civil society, participants highlight negative needs satisfiers such as fossil fuel dependency in transportations systems, limits to participation in democratic processes, privatisation of core infrastructures and services, and the corporate character of social media. The state is seen by

Table 4 Negative needs satisfiers by sites of degrowth transformations (selection)

	Civil society	State	Business
Material transactions with nature	Fossil fuel dependent and profit-driven transport system	Overall policy priority of economic growth Transport policies that complicate fossil-free ways of travelling	Monocultures
Social interactions between people	Limits of representative democracy undermining social participation	Reinforces representative democratic systems	Competitiveness
Social structures	Privatisation of core infrastructures/ basic services Standardised teaching practices in education system	Pension policies based on employment records	Growth imperative
Inner being	Corporate social media	Anthropocentrism Illusion of social differences as following from meritocratic principles	Perfectionism and productivity Anthropocentrism

the participants as prioritising economic growth, reinforcing representative democratic systems, pursuing employment-based pension policies and promoting anthropocentrism. Finally, as regards business, participants identified negative needs satisfiers such as producing food via monoculture and promoting the culture of competitiveness, growth orientation, perfectionism, productivity and anthropocentrism.

In contrast to the negative needs satisfiers, the positive needs satisfiers identified by the participants in the site of civil society include advertisement-free spaces, renewal of democracy via deliberative citizen forums, public and localised systems of non-commercial basic welfare provision, local currencies, and life-long learning. The state was envisioned by the participants as able to provide infrastructure for cycling and walking and life-long learning

Table 5 Positive needs satisfiers by sites of degrowth transformations (selection)

	Civil society	State	Business
Material transactions with nature	Advertisement-free zones	Infrastructure for cycling and walking	Sufficiency Localisation Sharing, repair and recycling economy
Social interactions between people	Democratic renewal via deliberative citizen forums	Introduce/strengthen deliberative elements in democratic institutions	Participatory budgeting
Social structures	Socialised/public and localised system of non-commercial basic welfare provision Local currencies	Life-long learning opportunities for all Universal basic income and universal basic services	Working time reduction
Inner being	Life-long learning Mindfulness, meditation	Decommodify/ socialise social media	Care

opportunities for all, and strengthen deliberative elements in democratic institutions and socialise social media. Positive needs satisfiers discussed by forum participants in relation to the site of business include sufficiency, localisation, participatory budgeting, reduction in working time and the ethic of care.

In conclusion

A considerable gap exists between what sustainability researchers regard as necessary behavioural changes to bring production and consumption patterns within planetary and social limits and what large portions of the Swedish population are currently prepared to undertake. Reforms designed to introduce/expand basic services are far more popular than reforms targeting the excessive lifestyles of the rich. This supports previous studies that have dealt with the ideological effect inherent in the capitalist mode of production. Not only economic categories but also social structures appear as natural and just (Koch 2018a). Targeting the wealth of rich citizens tends to be regarded as motivated by envy and is consequently rejected. This attitude is, however, not equally featured across social groups. Most people exhibit rather inconsistent habitus structures. Only a small minority is against degrowth transformations; a larger share of the Swedish population welcomes such change outright, whereas the vast majority is susceptible to some elements of bottom-up degrowth strategies while refusing others.

Future research could further explore group-specific habitus formations in relation to various aspects of degrowth transformations along the four planes of being in the sites of civil society, state and business. Such theoretically guided empirical contributions potentially constitute important pursuits in addressing different segments of the population in 'tailor-made' ways. Such studies could also be relevant in other countries and provide comparative data.

Citizen forums and similar deliberative methods are useful in bringing academic and practical knowledge together. The experiences of the Swedish forums suggest that it is possible to create conditions where people feel free to critically reflect on their life, nature, economy and society and share their thoughts. Even a superficial consideration of the positive needs satisfiers in Table 5 indicates the arrogance of the idea of leaving core societal tasks such as policymaking and planning exclusively to experts. The practical knowledge of the dwellers of local communities is indispensable when co-creating livelihoods with the potential of bringing production and consumption patterns within planetary boundaries while satisfying human needs. We can only speculate as to whether the public support for the suggested eco-social policies in Table 2 would increase if a significantly greater share of the population partook in similar deliberative forums and had a chance to collectively reflect. Governments could support such participatory exercises by enhancing the status of citizen forums and giving them advisory character. This would echo a range of degrowth proposals for more direct democracy.

Notes

1 Conversely, environmental and social activists sometimes underestimate the structural power asymmetries they are up against. The results may include extreme stress and burn-out experiences.

2 The percentage of Swedish residents who are concerned about both welfare and environmental issues is comparatively high. More than in other EU countries, they tend to be supportive of sustainable welfare and eco-social policies (Fritz and Koch 2019; Otto and Gugushvili 2020; Zimmermann and Graziano 2020; Emilsson 2022). We therefore consider Sweden an appropriate case to study people's susceptibility to degrowth transformations.

3 The final response rate of the survey study was 32% (951 out of 3,000 respondents). See Lee et al. (2023) for more detailed information on data material and representativity, survey methodology and additional results.

4 The overall response rate in this survey was 31%, that is, 1,529 out of 5,000 (see Fritz et al. 2021, Emilsson 2022 and Khan et al. 2022 for more details on data material and representativity, survey strategy and additional results).

5 In the 2021 survey the maximum income was set at 2 million euros per year and person, beyond which 100% taxation would kick in.

6 There are sizeable shares of respondents that neither consider the proposals positively nor negatively ('undecided'). One possible explanation is a lack of more detailed information as to how these policy reforms are to be applied – how they would be funded, which regulatory frameworks may be used/created among many other issues – and with what outcomes. Another possibility is that some of these proposals are simply too novel and/or radical for the respondents to take any stance. The idea of a maximum income, for example, is not promoted by any political party in Sweden. If this situation changed, it is conceivable that support rates would increase.

7 This position is typically represented by Louis Althusser's Marxist and Lévy-Strauss's anthropological structuralisms, Émile Durkheim and Talcott Parsons' functionalisms and Niklas Luhmann's system theory.

8 For this 'bottom-up' approach stand sociologists as different as Erving Goffman, George Herbert Mead and Herbert Blumer, as well as Jean-Paul Sartre's philosophy.

9 Hence, the insistence on social structures and, as a corollary, statistical likelihoods for certain preferences to be expressed by certain groups, does not at all deny the distinct existences of human beings within these structures, nor the empirical cases where individuals develop different subjectivities within the same social background (Archer 2003).

10 Some of these dimensions have clear-cut literal oppositions that we made explicit such as 'self-transcendence' versus 'self-enhancement'. In relation to other dimensions such as 'power and control' there are no direct oppositional terms. Habitus types were constructed according to the combined scores on these dimensions.

11 This share may of course be somewhat larger or smaller in other countries but is unlikely to be a majority.

12 For methodological details and further forum results from the project Sustainable Welfare for a New Generation of Social Policy, see Lindellee et al. (2021), Koch et al. (2021) and Lee et al. (2023).

Conclusion: the four planes of degrowth

In the preceding chapters, we have unfolded a theoretical perspective on degrowth transformations. We contend that for degrowth to materialise on a societal level, it requires transformations so comprehensive that no single actor, no single type of process, and no single type of mechanism will suffice to bring it about. In a nutshell, then, the perspective suggests that for degrowth transformations to occur, actions in the sites of civil society, business and the state are necessary – and they are necessary also on all scales, including the local, the national and the transnational. For degrowth to materialise, in other words, activities of agents positioned everywhere are required. In conceptualising degrowth in terms of deep transformations, we also highlight that it would necessitate profound changes on all planes of social being: (a) material transactions with nature, (b) social interactions between people, (c) social structure and (d) people's inner being (Bhaskar 1986, 1993).

In this concluding chapter, we connect a number of the key arguments made in previous chapters and expand on our perspective on degrowth transformations by relating it more systematically to the four planes model. In this context, we propose a new, holistic definition of degrowth. We also elaborate on the view of human beings underpinning our perspective before we end the book by identifying various issues meriting further contemplation and dialogue.

Less and more: on the dialectics of reduction and growth

Unsurprisingly, given the name that was chosen for it, degrowth is widely associated with reduction, with *less*.[1] This is unfortunate, because while degrowth is indeed about reducing various aspects of what currently exists, it is just as much about expanding other aspects. Degrowth is, in other words, also about *more*. Proponents of degrowth frequently call for growth in wellbeing (Hickel 2020), specific economic sectors (Jackson 2016), moral agency (Nesterova 2021c) and social justice (Demaria et al. 2013). Further to the distinction made between positive and negative needs satisfiers (Chapter 7), degrowth can be seen to entail both less and more on all the four aforementioned planes of being (Buch-Hansen and Nesterova 2023). In what follows, we first look at features that would need to be reduced on the various planes before turning to an elaboration of what would need to grow.

The early chapters of the book outlined how capitalism has adverse effects on all planes of social being. The capitalist organisation of societies and the capitalist growth imperative shape humans' *material transactions with nature*. Under capitalism, nature is exploited, commercialised, reshaped and destroyed more than under any other economic system. Against this, degrowth aims for a considerably smaller throughput of matter and energy, with reduced greenhouse gas emissions and less waste and pollution. This outcome is to be accomplished via, for example, less production and consumption of unnecessary goods and services, less flying and fewer transportation miles (Hassler et al. 2019; Trainer 2012). Prerequisites for these and other reductions in the ecological footprints of humans, especially materially privileged ones, include a less exploitative and instrumentalist approach towards nature (Næss 1990) and that nature is to a far smaller extent transformed into industrial sites (such as monoculture plantations of food crops and forests) and built environments (Nesterova 2022a).

Capitalist structures shape *social interactions* between humans, as a result of which they come to be based on, for example, antagonism, competitiveness, instrumentalism and alienation. Degrowth entails that interactions come to be shaped less by these and other intersubjective attitudes and features, including, for example, racism, sexism, intolerance and climate change denial. Capitalist *social structures* also produce hierarchies and deep inequalities within and between societies. Degrowth implies less competition among companies and other organisations as well as among individuals. It also implies moving towards socio-economic systems on all scales with reduced social and economic inequalities, fewer hierarchies and less bureaucracy. This would involve, for instance, state steering different from the types prevailing in contemporary capitalism. For example, powers could be delegated from the national to the local scale, the idea being that this is the scale at which citizens could come to directly participate in shaping various policies affecting them (Chapter 5). Finally, while people are impacted differently by capitalism and internalise social structures differently (as seen in the analysis of habitus types in Chapter 7), capitalist structures instil greed and egoism in the *inner being* of humans, contributing to nurturing the mode of having orientation (Fromm 2013) towards the world. Degrowth, to the contrary, implies an altogether different outlook, that most people become less egocentric, entitled and hedonistic.

Bhaskar's diagnosis was that our world finds itself in crises on all the various planes (Bhaskar 2016). On top of the ecological crisis on plane (a), the crisis of democracy on plane (b) and the inequality crisis on plane (c), comes an existential crisis on plane (d). While this is certainly a gloomy diagnosis, in a sense it does not capture the depth of the current crisis. That is, not only does the world confront a crisis on each plane, several intertwined, and mutually reinforcing, crises exist on each plane and across the planes. To give but one example, the climate and biodiversity crises unfolding on plane (a) amplify one another and have ramifications such as mental health issues on plane (d) (Cianconi et al. 2020). It follows from what was said in the preceding paragraphs that, seen from the vantage point of degrowth, the capitalist organisation of society and the capitalist growth imperative constitute direct or indirect causes of most of the aspects of contemporary societies that need to be reduced or altogether abolished if an eco-social collapse is to be avoided.

Yet as we observed above, degrowth is also about growth, expansion, more. Indeed, it is helpful to see reduction as standing in a dialectical relationship with growth. A smaller throughput of matter and energy (plane [a]) requires not only various forms of reduction, it also necessitates that *more* clean energy forms are used and that more behaviour comes to be informed by respect and regard for non-human beings, biodiversity and life (Næss 1990). This involves, for instance, that more economic activities become more nature- and place-based, that increasingly the specific constellations of natural structures existing in specific locations are taken into consideration (Nesterova 2022b). If social interactions (plane [b]) are to be premised less on antagonism, they need instead to become based *more* on values and principles such as tolerance of diversity, respect and concern for others, empathy, sufficiency, gentleness and care. If social structures are to involve fewer hierarchies, deep inequalities and competition, they need instead to involve *more* flat hierarchies and a more equal distribution of economic and other resources, as well as more collaborative relations (plane [c]). Finally, if the mode of having is to become less prevalent, substantial inner growth is required (plane [d]) so that the mode of being can become more prevalent (Fromm 2013). Most people would need to change themselves, becoming *more* attuned to joy, reflection and mindfulness, becoming more capable of feeling oneness with the world as a whole (cf. Fromm 2022; Næss 1990). In Table 6 we summarise some of the items on the four planes that would entail reduction or growth with degrowth; additional less and more items can be found in the analysis of, respectively, negative and positive needs satisfiers in Chapter 7.

Table 6 Less and more on four planes

	Less	More
(a) Material transactions with nature	Matter and energy throughput, extractivism and instrumental treatment of nature, waste, pollution, greenhouse gas emissions, production and consumption of unnecessary goods, transportation/food miles, built environments	Cleaner energy forms, regard for nature, preservation of biodiversity and life, place-sensitivity, place-based activities/localisation, nature-based economic activities
(b) Social interactions	Competitiveness, greed, individualism, intolerance, racism, sexism, climate change denial, homophobia, xenophobia, hate, fear, alienation, instrumental treatment of humans	Empathy, compassion, peacefulness, solidarity, sufficiency, kindness, generosity and tolerance of diversity, spontaneous right action, fellow-feeling, respect and concern for others, care, mutual learning, democracy
(c) Social structures	Growth imperative, competition, inequality, patriarchy, rigid hierarchies, bureaucracy, structures of oppression, exploitation, domination, poverty, suffering	Collaboration, equal distribution of economic and other resources, flat hierarchies
(d) Inner being	Egoism and ego-realisation, egocentrism, equating the ego with the self, short-term orientation, entitlement, possessiveness and materialism ('to have'), hedonism	Love, creativity, oneness, gentleness towards being and beings, awareness, curiosity, transcending the narrow ego/self, seeing oneself as part of the broader existence, self-realisation, fulfilment, harmony, joy ('to be')

Source: Buch-Hansen and Nesterova (2023).

An advantage of our 'less and more perspective' is its ability to highlight that, although it implies deep transformations on all four planes, degrowth would still build on forms, practices, ideas and values that already exist. Indeed, everything in the 'more' column in the above table already exists. For example, multiple degrowth-compatible initiatives, movements and modes of being already can be found alongside or even within capitalist economies, as well as alongside consumer societies (Burkhart et al. 2020; Gibson-Graham and Dombroski 2020). Yet they do not yet exist on the necessary scale. It is paramount for degrowth practice and research to identify niches of such initiatives and modes of being and identify the structural preconditions within which they may be expanded to become 'dominant' in their own right.

A related advantage of the perspective is that it makes it possible to avoid viewing degrowth in overly crude and reductionist terms. We come back to other aspects of this below, but one aspect is that it becomes clearer that it is not the case that what currently exists will entirely disappear so that something entirely new can appear instead. Just as the items in the more column to a (typically limited) extent exist in contemporary capitalism, so the items in the less column would not right away, if at all, be obliterated in a degrowth society. For example, a certain matter and energy throughput is an inevitable part of human existence and activity. Still, degrowth transformations would entail that the balance tips decisively in favour of the items in the more column.

In Chapter 3 we pointed to various prerequisites for degrowth to materialise on a wide scale. Building on political economy scholarship, we identified a major crisis as a first prerequisite, noting that currently capitalism finds itself if not in a systemic crisis, then certainly in a multidimensional structural crisis. As a second prerequisite we pointed to the need for a political project that can inform political decision-making, suggesting that at least in some important respects degrowth may be considered such a project. In this context we pointed to some of the many policies that are being discussed in degrowth circles. A third prerequisite we identified was the mobilisation of a comprehensive coalition of social forces (a power bloc) pushing for degrowth. We suggested that currently no coalition powerful enough to bring about degrowth exists. We also noted that whereas coalitions are typically analysed in class-based terms in political economy scholarship, degrowth entails transformations of a depth and magnitude necessitating the combined actions of myriad actors positioned in states, civil society and business. Indeed, just as transformations would require democratically adopted policies implemented by local, national and transnational state apparatuses, so they would require a wide range of bottom-up civil society and business initiatives on the same scales.

As a final prerequisite for degrowth transformations, we highlighted the need for widespread popular consent to it, something that currently also does not exist. We observed that such consent would require self-transformation at the level of the individual, involving that people come to view degrowth as something desirable and a sensible development. In the absence of such self-transformation, it is difficult to imagine the rise of a pro-degrowth comprehensive coalition of social forces and electoral majorities consenting to degrowth policies. Importantly, as the analysis of data collected in Sweden shows, not all degrowth policies are equally (un)popular. Moreover, different habitus groups exhibit different degrees of susceptibility to degrowth policies on the various planes of being (Chapter 7).

In our view, for degrowth to materialise on the four planes, pervasive and sustained *gentleness and care* for and towards non-human beings and nature, other people, society and one's inner being are required. In other words, we see gentleness and care as underlying principles that can guide transformations across the various planes (Buch-Hansen 2021). As we understand it, *gentleness* involves a felt sensitivity to the condition and suffering of humans and non-humans (Bhaskar 1993; Sayer 2011; Næss 1990), a reflective and genuine concern and intentional humanness and kindness towards being and beings manifested in our actions (see also Dufourmantelle 2018). As for care, we understand it 'as a species activity that includes everything that we do to maintain, continue, and repair our "world" so that we can live in it as well as possible. That world includes our bodies, our selves, and our environment, all of which we seek to interweave in a complex, life-sustaining web' (Fisher and Tronto 1990: 40). Several scholars have pointed to care as an aspect of degrowth, highlighting, for example, care for nature and that care work should be recognised as work (Spash 1993; Dengler and Lang 2022). Yet we understand care to be at the heart of what degrowth transformations entail and regard it as an act or practice that is exercised when gentleness constitutes one's core attitude towards the world.

Further to the above observations, we conceptualise *degrowth* as deep transformations occurring on all four interrelated planes of social being, on different scales and in all sites, guided by gentleness and care, towards a society co-existing harmoniously within itself and with nature.

Plane thinking: avoiding reductionism and binaries

In thinking of degrowth transformations, and in practising degrowth, it is crucial to avoid reductionism, acknowledge the interconnectedness of the planes of being and to recognise diversity on each plane.

Reductionism with respect to the planes consists in giving primacy to one or more of them while excluding or downplaying the importance of the rest. Such reductionism should be avoided inasmuch as it leads to superficial and one-dimensional perspectives, as well as to problematic practices. For example, if human transactions with nature are regarded as the all-important plane, it may well result in the adoption of policies that inflict harm on the inner being of human beings. A proposal such as that to introduce 'birth permits' to control population growth (Daly 1991) would be a case in point. A similarly problematic, indeed distorted, perspective results from giving primacy to self-transformations on plane (d) of inner being to the exclusion of consideration of, say, the structural context within which such transformations are to unfold. The point here is that, in relation to degrowth as well as in relation to any social phenomenon, all four planes should be recognised as important.

Our point is not to suggest that all research needs to focus equally on each plane. It may well be the case that particular research questions make it relevant to focus on particular planes and not others. For example, research on institutional forms (Chapter 2) and the processes through which they come into being may focus less on planes (a) and (d) than on (b) and (c), that is, on social interactions and structures. Yet any institutional form exists and has effects on all the planes. For example, money – whether taking the form of physical notes and coins or being digital – entails consumption of matter and energy and thus involves transactions with nature. And the extent to which society and markets are organised around money cannot but affect subjectivities. As such, it is ultimately insufficient (reductionist) to analyse the monetary regime (or any other institutional form) in terms of only some of the planes.

Extant degrowth scholarship does typically focus on multiple planes, albeit without using the plane terminology. Nonetheless, there is also a clear tendency for it to focus mainly on certain planes, not least those of material transactions with nature (plane [a]) and social structure (plane [c]). The focus on the former plane is seen in, for instance, research dealing with questions related to the size of the economy and throughput of matter and energy, whereas the focus on the latter plane can be seen in, for instance, works focusing on the need to transcend capitalism and reduce economic inequality (e.g., Latouche 2009). In particular, the plane of inner being has received little attention, both in degrowth scholarship (Brossmann and Islar 2020) and sustainability research more generally (Ives et al. 2020; Woiwode et al. 2021). As we have alluded to several times in this book, this plane is no less important than the other planes – in fact it is essential to take it into consideration in relation to degrowth transformations. Deep changes, indeed massive growth, is needed on this plane.

It is also important to recognise the *interconnectedness* of the planes. Initiatives – be it in the site of civil society, the state, business or combinations thereof – resulting in desirable results on one plane do not necessarily also result in positive outcomes on other planes. Consider, for example, the well-known definition of degrowth according to which it is 'an equitable downscaling of production and consumption that increases human well-being and enhances ecological conditions at the local and global level' (Schneider et al. 2010: 511). By pointing to how changes on plane (a) result in positive changes on plane (d), this definition recognises the interrelatedness of planes. This image of downscaling being a process leading directly to a state of wellbeing is very common in the degrowth literature (e.g., Hickel 2020; Trainer 2020). Yet the question is how realistic this scenario is. On one hand, people would, hopefully, experience degrowth transformations as meaningful and pleasant in important respects. On the other hand, it seems very likely that giving up on the mode of having, adapting to a lifestyle with a small ecological footprint, would cause people to have all sorts of concerns and problems. Observing how moving towards the mode of being can be challenging, Fromm writes that ' "to be" requires giving up one's egocentricity and selfishness .... But most people find giving up their having orientation too difficult; any attempt to do so arouses their intense anxiety' (2013: 76–77). It should thus be recognised that it may well be the case that degrowth-desirable changes on plane (a), such as a downscaling of production and consumption, does not lead to immediately improved human wellbeing on plane (d) (see also Koch et al. 2017).

This point is vital to keep in mind when designing and implementing the various types of policies discussed in degrowth circles (Chapter 5). While these policies are generally meant to absent or reduce 'less' items while promoting the growth of 'more' items (Table 6), they may come to have positive effects on some planes and negative on others. When designing policies aimed to reduce humans' ecological footprint on plane (a), effects on the three other planes should be carefully considered. It should also be considered that the same policy may have both positive and negative effects on the same plane. For example, a policy leading to the outsourcing of dirty production or export of waste may improve material transactions with nature in one country while making them worse in other countries. Another example is caps on income and wealth. This policy instrument could constitute a potent way to simultaneously reduce economic inequality (plane [c]) and undermine the ability of rich people to lead environmentally unsustainable lifestyles (plane [a]). However, if the revenue from such caps is redistributed to those at the bottom of the income ladder, the result may well be that aggregate demand is stimulated, leading to environmentally harmful production, consumption and growth (plane [a]) (Buch-Hansen and Koch

2019). This suggests that it is necessary to not merely consider any particular policy in relation to each of the four planes, it is also necessary to consider the combined effects of different degrowth policy mixes.

Finally, it is important to recognise *diversity* on each plane (Nesterova 2022b). Unfortunately, when presenting visions of desired futures, much degrowth scholarship overlooks that not all individuals treasure the same forms of social interactions (plane [b]). This can be observed in, for instance, the context of visions centred around 'conviviality', a concept denoting that human beings enjoy one another's company while acting in solidarity (Liegey and Nelson 2020: 2). It is also common to see degrowth scholars treat human wellbeing in a narrow way, as something that will come about from living in eco-communities (Cattaneo 2015) or other small communities (Trainer 2020), as well as from engaging in activities like drama, meditation or craft workshops in community settings (Jackson and Victor 2013).

The problem with presenting degrowth visions in this manner is that people are different (plane [d]). Some thrive in settings with convivial interactions, decentralised decision-making, communal living and the like. Others, for a variety of reasons, by no means thrive in such contexts. For them, wellbeing may be associated with spending time alone or in smaller groups and/ or from engaging with non-human beings and features of nature, say trees and lakes. In articulating visions of degrowth futures it is thus important to recognise that wellbeing has different sources for different individuals, and that one form of life, say a convivial life in an ecovillage, is not necessarily better than another form of life, say a solitary mode of being (e.g., Thoreau 2016). This is the case in relation to degrowth transformations and it is the case in general. Degrowth, then, should not be equated with one specific life form.

Further to this, a nuanced perspective on degrowth transformations necessitates moving beyond crude binary thinking, that is, thinking in terms of opposites such as sustainable versus unsustainable, degrowth versus growth, all good versus all bad.[2] The problem with describing complex social processes and entities in such terms is that most processes and entities contain a mixture of positive and negative elements. For example, the same business can incorporate multiple degrowth-compatible and multiple unsustainable elements, and over time the constellation of these elements can change. It is also important to recognise that businesses operate under different conditions, which may hinder or facilitate their transformations. For example, the not-for-profit sector is subjected to different company laws in different settings, even in countries with similar legal traditions such as the Scandinavian countries (Gjems-Onstad 1996). Again, however, it is important not to equate not-for-profit businesses with degrowth, the reason being that such businesses – like for-profit businesses – may incorporate both degrowth-compatible and degrowth-incompatible elements (Chapter 6). The aforementioned less-and-more dialectic in many ways already exists within organisations as well as in human lives. Avoiding binary thinking brings the plurality of practices and complexity to the surface, making it possible to evaluate the different elements, seeing how each of them can become more in line with degrowth. Taking such an approach is less likely to alienate people, businesses and policymakers than the approach of setting up unrealistic and perfectionistic standards.

Further to the observation that settings differ, it is also important to recognise that neither degrowth policies nor policy mixes can or should be the same in different locations. There are at least two reasons for this. One is that policies that come into being via genuinely democratic processes are unlikely to be identical across different settings. The other is that for policies to have the desired effects, their design and implementation need to be tailored to the uniqueness of the natural and social settings, people and sectors they cover. To illustrate, the degrowth literature advocates small-scale organic farming instead of large-scale monoculture *and* it advocates work time reduction in the form of shorter workdays or workweeks. Yet it is important to recognise that organic farming involves working with nature in accordance with its rhythms rather than in accordance with a schedule. In some periods, intensive and extensive work is required; in other periods there is little work to do. As such, policies fixing daily, weekly or monthly work hours at a particular level could turn out highly counterproductive. Degrowth policies would also differ depending on the scales at which they are enacted. Some policies are suitable for the local scale, others for the national and still others for the transnational. For example, it is difficult to imagine how a cap on income and/or wealth could work properly in the absence of extensive transnational coordination.

Hope and humanism: why degrowth is going to happen

The scale and depth of the transformations needed for degrowth to happen are vast. Only if one adopts a particular view of human beings can it be assumed that such transformations, despite the various challenges associated with them, will come to be perceived as desirable and be sought after. This view is overall hopeful, positive and optimistic, corresponding largely to the ideas and ideals of humanism and fields which draw inspiration from it, such as humanistic psychology (Schneider et al. 2015) and humanistic geography (Tuan 2008). Humanism emphasises general human goodness and human potential for growth and self-realisation, while avoiding naively equating human goodness with sainthood or perfection. To assume general human goodness is not to say that humans are *only good*. Indeed, it is easy to find examples of the contrary, manifested in exploitation, aggression and violence towards fellow humans, non-humans and nature. Moreover, each human being is a unique individual. Importantly, the emphasis humanism places on humans does not entail anthropocentrism or a human-centric approach. Humanism considers it to be within human capacity to experience and enact concern and care towards other beings and nature (Pilisuk and Joy 2015).

Humanism equally honours our selfhood (but not egoism) and our ability to relate in a healthy and intentional manner with the self, others (fellow humans and non-humans) and nature. It highlights our human capacities for intentionality, creativity, love, benevolence, fellow-feeling, empathy, concern and care, as well as our ability, and even inherent need, for growth in relation to each of those capacities and development as persons. This holistic development, made possible by our human nature (Chapter 1), is self-transformation. In our view, such self-transformation, though not sufficient, is necessary for degrowth to materialise. We intentionally avoid singling out any particular group of agents such as businesspersons or politicians who need to self-transform. Instead, we suggest that self-transformation should be a wish, commitment and activity of all humans irrespective of their roles within societies.

The possibility of self-transformation creates the sense of hope that a harmonious, peaceful and long-term coexistence between humans and nature, and within humanity, is possible. Self-transformation can be brought about via a variety of mechanisms relating to the self, others and nature. In terms of the self, it is helpful to view personal growth as a meaningful and 'life-long process' (Cassis and Birchmore 1985: 38). Personal growth is self-transformative when it aims at humanist ideals of creativity, love, freedom, empathy, fellow-feeling, kindness, joy and others. Otherwise, it is illusory, or is a personal decline, if it is aimed at accumulation, status and other manifestations of the 'mode of having' (Fromm 2013).

Importantly, personal growth is not only a matter of learning about different modes of being and outlining an ecological worldview, but a matter of living this worldview, bringing it into one's everyday practice. Indeed, a 'person can no more learn about humanism by reading about it than he can learn about music, painting, or teaching by intellectual effort alone. They must all be experienced to be known' (Robinson 1977: 636). Since degrowth is an inherently ecological vision of the future which is acutely mindful of our interconnection with nature, nurturing one's relationship with nature is essential. Connection with nature is self-transformative and helps humans transcend the feeling of meaninglessness and emptiness of being in a technological and consumerist society (May 2009). Apart from nature, relating with others can provide opportunities for working together towards a degrowth future: the scale of transformation required for degrowth is only achievable if the effort is collective. Yet the notion of 'others' does not have to be limited to humans or 'others of my kind' (Heidegger 2001: 156). Being with more-than-human others such as trees, mountains and rivers can provide inspiration for self-transformations (Softas-Nall and Woody 2017) and a sense of desire to preserve other beings, their future generations and their habitats (Regan 1981).

Self-transformations unfold within the frameworks of social systems and structures. Fromm (2013: 8) observed that 'a change of the human heart is possible only to the extent that drastic economic and social changes occur that give the human heart the chance for change and the courage and the vision to achieve it'. While it appears natural to emphasise the self and its becoming when discussing self-transformations, it is thus important to contemplate structural mechanisms which can facilitate growth on the plane of inner being. Such mechanisms can be, for instance, a transformed system of education which is orientated towards personal growth and non-utilitarian and non-anthropocentric philosophies, and eco-social policies which create spaces and opportunities for such growth. Throughout the book, we have offered multiple examples of such policies.

Towards new dialogues

Reflecting on all-encompassing and deep transformations is an interdisciplinary endeavour. In this book, multiple fields of knowledge such as philosophy, political economy, sociology and geography, which are outside the traditional disciplinary groundings of degrowth (that is, ecological economics and political ecology), have provided inspiration and made possible a deep and holistic theorisation of degrowth transformations. However, many possibilities for further unfolding our understanding of degrowth transformations remain. While acknowledging that it is impossible to fully capture and outline the multitude of interdisciplinary dialogues that could take place and be fruitful, in what follows we end the book by indicating some pathways for further investigations. We focus particularly on some of the loose ends of contemplations contained in this book.

In terms of pathways for further research, we invite investigations of problematic and uncomfortable areas where the somewhat idealistic vision of degrowth meets the existing structures of the real world. Such problematic areas include, for instance, the question of large businesses and long supply chains, and questions of technology and our societies' overwhelming reliance on it. Not only is it difficult to imagine the human world functioning while relying on small-scale production and lower technologies, but also the services and technologies which degrowth celebrates (for example, railway travel, modern healthcare and education) inherently rely on large-scale production and service provision, large businesses and global supply chains. Moreover, it may be the case that the ambitious objective of degrowth to reduce matter and energy throughput requires the use of technology to collect and monitor data. The extent to which the large-scale and global reductions envisioned by degrowth proponents are accomplished should not be merely intuitive: while transformations should be motivated by a deeply transformed worldview and ethic, measurement of progress towards them is necessary. Another problematic area deserving far more attention is the legal aspects of degrowth. That is, many questions remain unanswered with respect to the legal implications of degrowth transformations and with respect to what degrowth-facilitating regulations and legislations may look like on different scales, in different places, and for different sites.

It appears timely to engage in more serious dialogues with other sustainability fields and ideas such as circular economy and strong sustainability. While ideological, political and philosophical differences between, say, degrowth and circular economy exist, the common desire for a genuinely sustainable society can provide a starting point for fruitful collaborations (Dzhenghiz et al. 2023; Nesterova and Buch-Hansen 2023; Savini 2023). Circular economy can assist the efforts of degrowth researchers by providing insights into processes and designs which can help achieve more sustainable modes of production and service provision, as well as cases of concrete industries and examples of legislation. Equally productive dialogues can take place between degrowth and fields of knowledge which share with degrowth a deep appreciation of, and care towards, nature and the need for individual humans and humanity in general to relate with nature differently. Ecopsychology (e.g., Roszak et al. 1995) and humanistic psychology (e.g., Schneider et al. 2015) are such fields.

While in this book we have adopted a critical realist perspective as our philosophical grounding and commitment, other philosophies may shed light on deep transformations and open new spaces for new methodologies (ethnographies, sensory and embodied methods etc.) and new lines of inquiry. For instance, degrowth traditionally focused on human wellbeing and mostly included non-humans under the label of nature. New materialism (see e.g., Coole and Frost 2010; Gamble et al. 2019) can provide an alternative perspective via its focus on agency of matter and more-than-human beings. Deep ecology (Næss 2016; Sessions 1995) likewise emphasises our unavoidable connectedness with nature and places, and our own materiality, and encourages us to consider, and relate with, other forms of life and respect their right to self-realisation. Finally, scholarship on degrowth transformations could benefit from entering dialogues with other perspectives in the philosophy of science, constructionism and (moderated) positivism being cases in point (Buch-Hansen and Nesterova 2021; see also Buch-Hansen 2022).

Apart from new ideas and contents which new dialogues may engage with and create, it is our hope that new dialogues will emerge in, and in relation to, other places and contexts. In this book, as well as in our everyday research practice, we emphasise place-sensitivity. Thus, much of our research, including the research reported in this book, is done in Europe and more specifically in the Nordics. We invite others to apply the same and other parts of the perspective we have unfolded here in empirical and comparative empirical studies in other locations.

While indeed our intention in this section is to present possibilities for new dialogues in relation to ideas and disciplines, we also emphasise that a new attitude to such dialogues appears timely. An appropriate guiding ethos for genuine dialogues and collaborations between degrowth and other fields can be what Gibson-Graham (2003: 67) calls ethos of engagement: 'An ethos of engagement is an aspect of a politics of becoming, where subjects are made anew through engaging with others. This transformative process involves cultivating generosity in the place of hostility and suspicion.' Actively and intentionally cultivating generosity, engaging in teamwork despite perceived differences, and thinking together are essential. After all, deep transformations are not merely a theory of how changes (could) unfold; they are a practice of (de)growth.

Notes

1 The present and the next section draw on Buch-Hansen and Nesterova (2023).
2 Some events, attitudes and practices cannot be part of degrowth, a case in point being violence directed towards humans, non-humans and nature.

References

Adloff, F. (2021) 'Capitalism and civil society revisited or: Conceptualizing a civil, sustainable and solidary economy'. *International Journal of Politics, Culture, and Society*, 34:2, 149–159.

Adorno, T. W., Frenkel-Brunswik, E., Levinson, D. J., and Sanford, R. N. (1950) *The Authoritarian Personality*. New York: Harper and Row.

Alexander, S., and Gleeson, B. (2022) 'Collective sufficiency: Degrowth as a political project'. In S. Alexander, S. Chandrashekeran, and B. Gleeson (eds), *Post-Capitalist Futures. Paradigms, Politics, and Prospects*. New York: Palgrave, 53–64.

Amable, B. (2000) 'Institutional complementarity and diversity of social systems of innovation and production'. *Review of International Political Economy*, 7:4, 645–687.

Amable, B., and Palombarini, S. (2009) 'A neorealist approach to institutional change and the diversity of capitalism'. *Socio-Economic Review*, 7:1, 123–143.

Archer, M. S. (1995) *Realist Social Theory: The Morphogenetic Approach*. Cambridge: Cambridge University Press.

Archer, M. S. (2003) *Structure, Agency, and the Internal Conversation*. Cambridge: Cambridge University Press.

Arts, W., and Gelissen, J. (2002) 'Three worlds of welfare capitalism or more? A state-of-the-art report'. *Journal of European Social Policy*, 12:2, 137–158.

Atkinson, W. (2019) 'Time for Bourdieu: Insights and oversights'. *Time and Society*, 28:3, 951–970.

Babić, M. (2023) *The Rise of State Capital: Transforming Markets and International Politics*. Newcastle-upon-Tyne: Agenda.

Babic, M., and Sharma, S. E. (2023) 'Mobilising critical international political economy for the age of climate breakdown'. *New Political Economy*, 28:5, 758–779.

Baccaro, L., and Howell, C. (2017) *Trajectories of Neoliberal Transformation: European Industrial Relations Since the 1970s*. Cambridge: Cambridge University Press.

Bailey, D. (2015) 'The environmental paradox of the welfare state: The dynamics of sustainability'. *New Political Economy*, 20:6, 793–811.

Barca, S. (2019) 'The labor(s) of degrowth'. *Capitalism Nature Socialism*, 30:2, 207–216.

Barca, S., Chertkovskaya, E., and Paulsson, A. (2019) 'The end of political economy as we knew it? From growth realism to nomadic utopianism'. In E. Chertkovskaya, A. Paulsson and S. Barca (eds), *Towards a Political Economy of Degrowth*. London: Rowman and Littlefield, 1–18.

Barlow, N., Regen, L., Cadiou, N., Chertkovskaya, E., Hollweg, M., Plank, C., Schulken, M. and Wolf, V. (eds) (2022) *Degrowth and Strategy. How to Bring About Social-Ecological Transformation*. London: Mayfly, 342–365.

Bärnthaler, R. (2023) 'Degrowth and strategy: A critique and ways forward'. Available at SSRN: https://ssrn.com/abstract=4352024 (accessed 31 May 2023).

Bauwens, T. (2021) 'Are the circular economy and economic growth compatible? A case for post-growth circularity'. *Resources, Conservation and Recycling*, 175, 1–3.

Becker, C. (2006) 'The human actor in ecological economics: Philosophical approach and research perspectives'. *Ecological Economics*, 60, 17–23.

Becker, J., and Raza, W. (2000) 'Theory of regulation and political ecology: An inevitable separation?' *Économie et Sociétés*, 11, 55–70.

Benton, T. (2001) 'Why are sociologists naturephobes?' In J. Lopez and G. Potter (eds), *After Postmodernism: An Introduction to Critical Realism*. London: Athlone, 133–145.

Bhaskar, R. (1986) *Scientific Realism and Human Emancipation*. London: Verso.

Bhaskar, R. (1989) *Reclaiming Reality: A Critical Introduction to Contemporary Philosophy*. London: Verso.

Bhaskar, R. (1993) *Dialectic: The Pulse of Freedom*. London: Verso.

Bhaskar, R. (1998) *The Possibility of Naturalism: A Philosophical Critique of the Contemporary Human Sciences*, 3rd ed. London: Routledge.

Bhaskar, R. (2008) *A Realist Theory of Science*. London: Routledge.

Bhaskar, R. (2012a) *The Philosophy of MetaReality: Creativity, Love and Freedom*. London: Routledge.

Bhaskar, R. (2012b) *Reflections on MetaReality: Transcendence, Emancipation and Everyday Life*. London: Routledge.

Bhaskar, R. (2012c) 'Critical realism in resonance with Nordic ecophilosophy'. In R. Bhaskar, K. G. Høyer and P. Næss (eds), *Ecophilosophy in a World of Crisis: Critical Realism and the Nordic Contributions*. London: Routledge, 9–24.

Bhaskar, R. (2016) *Enlightened Common Sense. The Philosophy of Critical Realism*. London: Routledge.

Bhaskar, R. (2020) 'Critical realism and the ontology of persons'. *Journal of Critical Realism*, 19:2, 113–120.

Bhaskar, R., Frank, C., Høyer, K. G., Næss, P. and Parker, J. (eds) (2010) *Interdisciplinarity and Climate Change: Transforming Knowledge and Practice for our Global Future*. London: Routledge.

Bhaskar, R., Høyer, K. G., and Næss, P. (eds) (2012) *Ecophilosophy in a World of Crisis: Critical Realism and the Nordic Contributions*. London: Routledge.

Bieler, A. (2021) *Fighting for Water: Resisting Privatization in Europe*. London: Bloomsbury.

Bohle, D., and Greskovits, B. (2007) 'Neoliberalism, embedded neoliberalism and neocorporatism: Towards transnational capitalism in Central-Eastern Europe'. *West European Politics*, 30:3, 443–466.

Bohnenberger, K. (2020) 'Money, vouchers, public infrastructures? A framework for sustainable welfare benefits'. *Sustainability*, 12:2, 596.

Bohnenberger, K. (2022) 'Is it a green or brown job? A taxonomy of sustainable employment'. *Ecological Economics*, 200, 107469.

Bonnedahl, K. J., and Heikkurinen, P. (2019) 'The case for strong sustainability'. In K. J. Bonnedahl and P. Heikkurinen (eds), *Strongly Sustainable Societies: Organising Human Activities on a Hot and Full Earth*. London: Routledge, 1–20.

Boss, M. (1988) 'Recent considerations in daseinsanalysis'. *The Humanistic Psychologist*, 16:1, 58–74.

Bourdieu, P. (1984) *Distinction: A Social Critique of Judgement and Taste*. Cambridge, MA: Harvard University Press.

Bourdieu, P. (1990) *The Logic of Practice*. Cambridge: Polity.

Bourdieu, P. (1993) *Sociology in Question*. London: Sage.

Bourdieu, P. (1994) 'Rethinking the state: Genesis and structure of the bureaucratic field'. *Sociological Theory*, 12:1, 1–18.

Bourdieu, P. (1998) *Practical Reason*. Cambridge: Polity.

Bourdieu, P. (2000) *Pascalian Meditations*. Cambridge: Cambridge University Press.

Bourdieu, P. (2014) *On the State. Lectures at the Collège de France 1989–1992*. Cambridge: Polity.

Bourdieu, P., and Passeron, J.-C. (1977) *Reproduction in Education, Society and Culture*. London: Sage.

Boyer, R. (1990) *The Regulation School: A Critical Introduction*. New York: Columbia University Press.

Boyer, R., and Saillard, Y. (2002) 'A summary of regulation theory'. In R. Boyer and Y. Saillard (eds), *Regulation Theory: The State of the Art*. London: Routledge, 36–44.

Brand, U., and Wissen, M. (2012) 'Global environmental politics and the imperial mode of living: Articulations of state–capital relations in the multiple crisis'. *Globalizations*, 9:4, 547–560.

Brand, U., and Wissen, M. (2013) 'Crisis and continuity of capitalist society-nature relationships: The imperial mode of living and the limits to environmental governance'. *Review of International Political Economy*, 20:4, 687–711.

Brand, U., Görg, C., and Wissen, M. (2011) 'Second order condensations of societal power relations: Environmental politics and internationalization of the state from a neo-poulantzian perspective'. *Antipode*, 43:1, 149–175.

Brandstedt, E., and Emmelin, M. (2016) 'The concept of sustainable welfare'. In M. Koch and O. Mont (eds), *Sustainability and the Political Economy of Welfare*. London: Routledge, 15–43.

Bremer, H., and Teiwes-Kügler, C. (2013) 'Habitusanalyse als habitus-hermeneutik'. *Zeitschrift für qualitative Sozialforschung*, 2, 199–219.

Brenner, N., Peck, J., and Theodore, N. (2010) 'After neoliberalization?' *Globalizations*, 7:3, 327–345.

Brossmann, J., and Islar, M. (2020) 'Living degrowth? Investigating degrowth practices through performative methods'. *Sustainability Science*, 15:3, 917–930.

Bruff, I. (2014) 'The rise of authoritarian neoliberalism'. *Rethinking Marxism*, 26:1, 113–129.

Buch-Hansen, H. (2014) 'Capitalist diversity and de-growth trajectories to steady-state economies'. *Ecological Economics*, 106, 167–173.

Buch-Hansen, H. (2018) 'The prerequisites for a degrowth paradigm shift: Insights from critical political economy'. *Ecological Economics*, 146, 157–163.

Buch-Hansen, H. (2021) 'Modvækst som paradigme, politisk projekt og bevægelse'. *Nyt fokus: Fra økonomisk vækst til bæredygtig udvikling*, 17 www.nytfokus.nu/ nummer-17/modvaekst-som-paradigme-politisk-projekt-og-bevaegelse/ (accessed 31 May 2023).

Buch-Hansen, H. (2022) 'Contending philosophy of social science perspectives: A flexible typology'. *Journal for the Theory of Social Behaviour*, 53:2, 183–199.

Buch-Hansen, H., and Carstensen, M. B. (2021) 'Paradigms and the political economy of ecopolitical projects: Green growth and degrowth compared'. *Competition and Change*, 25:3–4, 308–327.

Buch-Hansen, H., and Koch, M. (2019) 'Degrowth through income and wealth caps?' *Ecological Economics*, 160, 264–271.

Buch-Hansen, H., and Nesterova, I. (2021) 'Towards a science of deep transformations: Initiating a dialogue between degrowth and critical realism'. *Ecological Economics*, 190, 107188.

Buch-Hansen, H., and Nesterova, I. (2023) 'Less and more: Conceptualising degrowth transformations'. *Ecological Economics*, 205, 107731.

Buch-Hansen, H., and Nielsen, P. (2020) *Critical Realism: Basics and Beyond*. London: Bloomsbury.

Buch-Hansen, H., and Wigger, A. (2011) *The Politics of European Competition Regulation: A Critical Political Economy Perspective*. London: Routledge.

Buch-Hansen, H., Pissin, A., and Kennedy, E. (2016) 'Transitions towards degrowth and sustainable welfare: Carbon emission reduction and wealth and income distribution in France, the US and China'. In M. Koch and O. Mont (eds), *Sustainability and the Political Economy of Welfare*. London: Routledge, 143–157.

Büchs, M. (2021) 'Sustainable welfare: How do universal basic income and universal basic services compare?' *Ecological Economics*, 189, 107152.

Büchs, M., and Koch, M. (2017) *Postgrowth and Wellbeing: Challenges to Sustainable Welfare*. New York: Springer.

Büchs, M., and Koch, M. (2019) 'Challenges for the degrowth transition: The debate about wellbeing'. *Futures*, 105, 155–65.

Bulfone, F. (2022) 'Industrial policy and comparative political economy: A literature review and research agenda'. *Competition and Change*, 27:1, 22–43.

Buller, A. (2022) *The Value of a Whale: On the Illusions of Green Capitalism*. Manchester: Manchester University Press.

Burkett, P. (1999) *Marx and Nature. A Red and Green Perspective*. New York: St. Martin's.

Burkhart, C., Schmelzer, M., and Treu, N. (2020) *Degrowth in Movement(s): Exploring Pathways for Transformation*. Winchester: Zero.

Cahen-Fourot, L. (2020) 'Contemporary capitalisms and their social relation to the environment'. *Ecological Economics*, 172, 106634.

Cahen-Fourot, L., Aigner, E., and Schneider, C. (2022) 'Money and finance. An overview of strategies for social-ecological transformation in the field of money and finance and the case of the Austrian Cooperative for the Common Good'. In N. Barlow, L. Regen, N. Cadiou, E. Chertkovskaya, M. Hollweg, C. Plank, M. Schulken and V. Wolf (eds), *Degrowth and Strategy. How to Bring about Social-Ecological Transformation*. London: Mayfly, 342–365.

Camus, A. (2005) *The Myth of Sisyphus*. London: Penguin Books.

Cassis, C., and Birchmore, D. (1985) 'Developing human potential – An awakening process'. *Canadian Journal of Public Health/Revue Canadienne de Santé Publique*, 76, 38–42.

Castree, N. (2008) 'Neoliberalising nature: The logics of deregulation and reregulation'. *Environment and Planning A*, 40:2, 131–152.

Cattaneo, C. (2015) 'Eco-communities'. In G. D'Alisa, F. Demaria and G. Kallis (eds), *Degrowth: A Vocabulary for a New Era*. London: Routledge, 165–168.

Ceballos, G., Ehrlich, P. R., Barnosky, A. D., García, A., Pringle, R. M., and Palmer, T. M. (2015) 'Accelerated modern human-induced species losses: Entering the sixth mass extinction'. *Science Advances*, 1:5, 1400253.

Cerny, P. G. (1997) 'Paradoxes of the competition state: The dynamics of political globalization'. *Government and Opposition*, 32:2, 251–274.

Chertkovskaya, E., and Paulsson, A. (2021) 'Countering corporate violence: Degrowth, ecosocialism and organising beyond the destructive forces of capitalism'. *Organization*, 28:3, 405–425.

Chertkovskaya, E., Paulsson, A., and Barca, S. (eds) (2019) *Towards a Political Economy of Degrowth*. London: Rowman and Littlefield.

Chomsky, N. (1999) *Noam Chomsky: The Common Good*. Chicago: Odonian.

Cianconi, P., Betrò, S., and Janiri, L. (2020) 'The impact of climate change on mental health: A systematic descriptive review'. *Frontiers in Psychiatry*, 11, 74.

Clarke, N. (2013) 'Locality and localism: A view from British Human Geography'. *Policy Studies*, 34:5–6, 492–507.

Collier, A. (2003) *In Defence of Objectivity and Other Essays: On Realism, Existentialism and Politics*. London: Routledge.

Collier, A. (2004) *Marx*. Oxford: Oneworld.

Concialdi, P. (2018) 'What does it mean to be rich? Some conceptual and empirical issues'. *European Journal of Social Security*, 20:1, 3–20.

Coole, D., and Frost, S. (eds) (2010) *New Materialisms: Ontology, Agency, and Politics*. Durham, NC: Duke University Press.

Coote, A., and Percy, A. (2020) *The Case for Universal Basic Services*. Cambridge: Polity.

Cosme, I., Santos, R., and O'Neill, D. (2017) 'Assessing the degrowth discourse: A review and analysis of academic degrowth policy proposals'. *Journal of Cleaner Production*, 149, 321–334.

Cox, R. W. (1987) *Production, Power and World Order*. New York: Columbia University Press.

Cox, R. W. (1999) 'Civil society at the turn of the millennium: Prospects for an alternative world order'. *Review of International Studies*, 25:1, 3–28.

Cresswell, T. (2009) 'Place'. In N. Thrift and R. Kitchen (eds), *International Encyclopedia of Human Geography*. Amsterdam: Elsevier, 169–177.

Crouch, C. (2016) 'The march towards post-democracy, ten years on'. *The Political Quarterly*, 87:1, 71–75.

Dale, G. (2012a) 'Critiques of growth in classical political economy: Mill's stationary state and a Marxian response'. *New Political Economy*, 18:3, 431–457.

Dale, G. (2012b) 'The growth paradigm: A critique'. *International Socialism*, 134, 55–88.

D'Alisa, G., and Kallis, G. (2020) 'Degrowth and the state'. *Ecological Economics*, 169, 106486.

Daly, H. E. (1991) *Steady-State Economics*. Washington, DC: Island.

Daly, H. E. (1996) *Beyond Growth*. Boston, MA: Beacon.

Daly, H. E., and Townsend, K. N. (eds) (1993) *Valuing the Earth: Economics, Ecology, Ethics*. London: MIT Press.

Danermark, B., Ekström, M., Jakobsen, L., and Karlsson, J. (2002) *Explaining Society: Critical Realism in the Social Sciences*. London: Routledge.

Dannreuther, C., and Petit, P. (2006) 'Post-Fordism, beyond national models: The main challenges for Regulation Theory'. *Competition and Change*, 10:2, 100–112.

de los Reyes, P., and Mulinari, D. (2020) 'Hegemonic feminism revisited: On the promises of intersectionality in times of the precarisation of life'. *NORA – Nordic Journal of Feminist and Gender Research*, 28:3, 183–196.

Demaria, F., Schneider, F., Sekulova, F., and Martinez-Alier, J. (2013) 'What is degrowth? From an activist slogan to a social movement'. *Environmental Values*, 22:2, 191–215.

Dengler, C., and Lang, M. (2022) 'Commoning care: Feminist degrowth visions for a socio-ecological transformation'. *Feminist Economics*, 28:1, 1–28.

Dengler, C., and Seebacher, L. M. (2019) 'What about the global south? Towards a feminist decolonial degrowth approach'. *Ecological Economics*, 157, 246–252.

Diehm, C. (2007) 'Identification with nature: What it is and why it matters'. *Ethics and the Environment*, 12:2, 1–22.

Dietz, R., and O'Neill, D. (2013) *Enough is Enough. Building a Sustainable Economy in a World of Finite Resources.* London: Earthscan.

Dietz, K., and Wissen, M. (2009) 'Kapitalismus und "natürliche Grenzen". Eine kritische Diskussion ökomarxistischer Zugänge zur ökologischen Krise'. *Prokla*, 39:3, 351–369.

Dittmer, K. (2013) 'Local currencies for purposive degrowth? A quality check of some proposals for changing money-as-usual'. *Journal of Cleaner Production*, 54, 3–13.

Dörry, S., and Schulz, C. (2022) 'Financing post-growth? Green financial products for changed logics of production'. In B. Lange, M. Hülz, B. Schmid and C. Schulz (eds), *Post-Growth Geographies*. Bielefeld: Transcript, 241–261.

Douai, A., and Montalban, M. (2012) 'Institutions and the environment: The case for a political socio-economy of environmental conflicts'. *Cambridge Journal of Economics*, 36, 1199–1220.

Doyal, L., and Gough, I. (1991) *A Theory of Human Need.* Basingstoke: Macmillan.

Drews, S., Savin, I., and van den Bergh, J. C. (2019) 'Opinion clusters in academic and public debates on growth-vs-environment'. *Ecological Economics*, 157, 141–155.

Dryzek, J. S., Downes, D., Hunold, C., Schlosberg, D., and Hernes, H-K. (2003) *Green States and Social Movements: Environmentalism in the United States, United Kingdom, Germany and Norway.* Oxford: Oxford University Press.

Dryzek, J. S. (2016) 'Institutions for the Anthropocene: Governance in a changing earth system'. *British Journal of Political Science*, 46:4, 937–956.

Dufourmantelle, A. (2018) *Power of Gentleness: Meditations on the Risk of Living.* New York: Fordham University Press.

Duit, A. (2016) 'The four faces of the environmental state: Environmental governance regimes in 28 countries'. *Environmental Politics*, 25:1, 69–91.

Duit, A., Feindt, P. H., and Meadowcroft, J. (2016) 'Greening leviathan: The rise of the environmental state'. *Environmental Politics*, 25:1, 1–23.

Dukelow, F., and Murphy, M. P. (2022) 'Building the future from the present: Imagining post-Growth, post-productivist ecosocial policy'. *Journal of Social Policy*, 51:3, 504–518.

Dzhenghiz, T., Miller, L., Ovaska, J. P., and Patala, S. (2023) 'Unpacking circular economy: A problematizing review'. *International Journal of Management Reviews*, 25:2, 270–296.

Dziwok, E., and Jäger, J. (2021) 'A classification of different approaches to green finance and green monetary policy'. *Sustainability*, 13:21, 11902.

Eckersley, R. (2004) *The Green State: Rethinking Democracy and Sovereignty*. London: MIT Press.

Ehrnström-Fuentes, M., and Biese, I. (2022) 'The act of (de/re) growing: Prefiguring alternative organizational landscapes of socioecological transformations'. *Human Relations*, 76:11, 1739–1766.

Elder-Vass, D. (2007) 'Reconciling Archer and Bourdieu in an emergentist theory of action'. *Sociological Theory*, 25:4, 325–346.

Elgin, D. (2013) 'Voluntary simplicity: A path to sustainable prosperity'. *Social Change Review*, 11:1, 69–84.

Elgin, D., and Mitchell, A. (1977) 'Voluntary simplicity'. *Planning Review*, 5:6, 13–15.

Emerson, R. W. (2009a) *Essays: First Series*. Auckland: Floating Press.

Emerson, R. W. (2009b) *Essays: Second Series*. Auckland: Floating Press.

Emilsson, K. (2022) 'Support for sustainable welfare: A study of public attitudes related to an eco-social agenda among Swedish residents'. (PhD thesis, Faculty of Social Sciences, Lund University.)

Eskelinen, T., and Wilen, K. (2019) 'Rethinking economic ontologies: From scarcity and market subjects to strong sustainability'. In K. J. Bonnedahl and P. Heikkurinen (eds), *Strongly Sustainable Societies: Organising Human Activities on a Hot and Full Earth*. London: Routledge, 40–57.

Esping-Andersen, G. (1990) *The Three Worlds of Welfare Capitalism*. Cambridge: Polity.

Fair Squared GmbH (2022) 'Principles'. Available at: www.fairsquared.com/en/fairsquared/principles/ (accessed 31 May 2023).

Feldmann, M. (2006) 'Emerging varieties of capitalism in transition countries: Industrial relations and wage bargaining in Estonia and Slovenia'. *Comparative Political Studies*, 39:7, 829–854.

Fisher, B., and Tronto, J. (1990) 'Toward a feminist theory of caring'. In E. K. Abel and M. Nelson (eds), *Circles of Care: Work and Identity in Women's Lives*. Albany: SUNY Press, 35–62.

Fitzpatrick, N., Parrique, T., and Cosme, I. (2022) 'Exploring degrowth policy proposals: A systematic mapping with thematic synthesis'. *Journal of Cleaner Production*, 365, 132764.

Foster, J. B., Clark, B., and York, R. (2010) *The Ecological Rift: Capitalism's War on the Earth*. New York: Monthly Review Press.

Frankl, V. E. (2006) *Man's Search for Meaning*. Boston, MA: Beacon.

Frieden, J. A. (2007) *Global Capitalism: Its Fall and Rise in the Twentieth Century*. New York: W.W. Norton.

Fritz, M., and Koch, M. (2016) 'Economic development and prosperity patterns around the world: Structural challenges for a global steady-state economy'. *Global Environmental Change*, 38, 41–48.

Fritz, M., and Koch, M. (2019) 'Public support for sustainable welfare compared: Links between attitudes towards climate and welfare policies'. *Sustainability*, 11:15, 4146.

Fritz, M., Koch, M., Johansson, H., Emilsson, K., Hildingsson, R., and Khan, J. (2021) 'Habitus and climate change: Exploring support and resistance to sustainable welfare and social-ecological transformations in Sweden'. *The British Journal of Sociology*, 72:4, 874–890.

Fromm, E. (1961) *Marx's Concept of Man*. New York: Frederick Ungar.

Fromm, E. (2013) *To Have or To Be?* London: Bloomsbury.

Fromm, E. (2022) *The Art of Being*. London: Robinson.

Gamble, C. N., Hanan, J. S., and Nail, T. (2019) 'What is new materialism?' *Angelaki*, 24:6, 111–134.

Genschel, P., and Seelkopf, L. (2015) 'The competition state'. In S. Leibfried, E. Huber, M. Lange, J. D. Levy, F. Nullmeier and J. D. Stephens (eds), *The Oxford Handbook of Transformations of the State*. Oxford: Oxford University Press, 237–252.

Georgescu-Roegen, N. (1971) *The Entropy Law and the Economics Process*. Cambridge, MA: Harvard University Press.

Gibson-Graham, J. K. (2003) 'An ethics of the local'. *Rethinking Marxism*, 15:1, 49–74.

Gibson-Graham, J. K. (2006) *The End of Capitalism (As We Knew it): A Feminist Critique of Political Economy*. Minneapolis: University of Minnesota Press.

Gibson-Graham, J. K., and Dombroski, K. (2020) 'Introduction to the handbook of diverse economies: Inventory as ethical intervention'. In *The Handbook of Diverse Economies*. Cheltenham: Edward Elgar, 1–24.

Gills, B., and Morgan, J. (2021) 'Teaching climate complacency: Mainstream economics textbooks and the need for transformation in economics education'. *Globalizations*, 18:7, 1189–1205.

Gjems-Onstad, O. (1996) 'The legal framework and taxation of Scandinavian non-profit organisations'. *Voluntas: International Journal of Voluntary and Nonprofit Organizations*, 7:2, 195–212.

Glyn, A., Hughes, A., Lipietz, A., and Singh, A. (1990) 'The rise and fall of the golden age'. In S. A. Marglin and J. B. Schor (eds), *The Golden Age of Capitalism. Reinterpreting the Postwar Experience*. Oxford: Clarendon.

Gordon, D., Edwards, D., and Reich, M. (1982) *Segmented Work, Divided Workers*. Cambridge: Cambridge University Press.

Görg, C. (2003) *Regulation der Naturverhältnisse. Zu einer kritischen Theorie der ökologischen Krise*. Münster: Westfälisches Dampfboot.

Görg, C., Brand, U., Haberl, H., Hummel, D., Jahn, T., and Lier, S. (2017) 'Challenges for social-ecological transformations: Contributions from social and political ecology'. *Sustainability*, 9, 1045.

Gorz, A. (1980) *Ecology as Politics*. London: Pluto.

Gorz, A. (1989) *Critique of Economic Reason*. London: Verso.

Gorz, A. (2012) *Capitalism, Socialism, Ecology*. London: Verso.

Gough, I. (2016) 'Welfare states and environmental states: A comparative analysis'. *Environmental Politics*, 25:1, 24–47.

Gough, I. (2017) *Heat, Greed and Human Need. Climate Change, Capitalism and Sustainable Wellbeing*. Cheltenham: Edward Elgar.

Gough, I. (2020) 'Defining floors and ceilings: The contribution of human needs theory'. *Sustainability: Science, Practice and Policy*, 16:1, 208–219.

Gough, I., Meadowcroft, J., Dryzek, J., Gerhards, J., Lengfeld, H., Markandya, A., and Ortiz, R. (2008) 'JESP symposium: Climate change and social policy'. *Journal of European Social Policy*, 18:4, 325–344.

Graeber, D. (2018) *Bullshit Jobs: A Theory*. New York: Simon and Schuster.

Gramsci, A. (1971) *Selections from Prison Notebooks*. London: Lawrence and Wishart.

Gready, P., and Robins, S. (2017) 'Rethinking civil society and transitional justice: Lessons from social movements and "new" civil society'. *The International Journal of Human Rights*, 21:7, 956–975.

Haberl, H., Wiedenhofer, D., Virág, D., Kalt, G., Plank, B., Brockway, P., ... and Creutzig, F. (2020) 'A systematic review of the evidence on decoupling of GDP, resource use and GHG emissions, part II: Synthesizing the insights'. *Environmental Research Letters*, 15:6, 065003.

Hägerstrand, T. (2012) 'Global and local'. In R. Bhaskar, K. G. Høyer and P. Næss (eds), *Ecophilosophy in a World of Crisis: Critical Realism and the Nordic Contributions*. London: Routledge, 126–134.

Hall, P. A., and Soskice, D. (eds) (2001) *Varieties of Capitalism: The Institutional Foundations of Comparative Advantage*. Oxford: Oxford University Press.

Hankammer S., Kleer, R., Mühl, L., and Euler, J. (2021) 'Principles for organizations approaching sustainable degrowth: Framework development and application to four B Corps'. *Journal of Cleaner Production*, 300, 126818.

Hartwig, M. (2007) *Dictionary of Critical Realism*. London: Routledge.

Harvey, D. (2005) *The New Imperialism*. Oxford: Oxford University Press.

Harvey, D. (2010) *The Enigma of Capital*. London: Profile.

Harvey, D. (2014) *Seventeen Contradictions and the End of Capitalism*. Oxford: Oxford University Press.

Hasselbalch, J., Kranke, M., and Chertkovskaya, E. (2023) 'Organizing for transformation: Post-growth in International Political Economy'. *Review of International Political Economy*, 30:5, 1621–1638.

Hassler, A., Dwarkasing, C., Reckmann, E., Sekulova, F., Schneider, F., Iniesta-Arianda, I., ... and Mingorría, S. (2019) *Degrowth of Aviation. Reducing Air Travel in a Just Way*. Austria: Stay Grounded.

Hausknost, D. (2020) 'The environmental state and the glass ceiling of transformation'. *Environmental Politics*, 29:1, 17–37.

Heidegger, M. (2001) *Being and Time*. Oxford: Blackwell.

Heikkurinen, P. (2018) 'Degrowth by means of technology? A treatise for an ethos of releasement'. *Journal of Cleaner Production*, 197, 1654–1665.

Heikkurinen, P., and Ruuska, T. (eds) (2021) *Sustainability Beyond Technology: Philosophy, Critique, and Implications for Human Organization*. Oxford: Oxford University Press.

Heikkurinen, P., Lozanoska, J., and Tosi, P. (2019) 'Activities of degrowth and political change'. *Journal of Cleaner Production*, 211, 555–565.

Hickel, J. (2020) *Less is More: How Degrowth will Save the World*. New York: Random House.

Hinton, J. (2020) 'Fit for purpose? The role of profit for sustainability'. *Journal of Political Ecology*, 27:1, 236–262.

Hirsch, F. (1976) *The Social Limits to Growth*. Cambridge, MA: Harvard University Press.

Hirvilammi, T. (2020) 'The virtuous circle of sustainable welfare as a transformative policy idea'. *Sustainability*, 12:1, 391.

Hirvilammi, T., and Koch, M. (2020) 'Sustainable welfare beyond growth'. *Sustainability*, 12:5, 1824.

Hirvilammi, T., Häikiö, L., Johansson, H., Koch, M., and Perkiö, J. (2023) 'Social policy in a climate emergency context: Towards an ecosocial research agenda'. *Journal of Social Policy*, 52:1, 1–23.

Hopkins, R. (2011) *The Transition Companion*. Devon: Green Books.

Hornborg, A. (2019) *Nature, Society, and Justice in the Anthropocene: Unravelling the Money-Energy-Technology Complex*. Cambridge: Cambridge University Press.

Howell, R. A. (2012) 'Living with a carbon allowance: The experiences of carbon rationing action groups and implications for policy'. *Energy Policy*, 41, 250–258.

Huizinga, J. (1950) *Homo Ludens: A Study of the Play-Element in Culture*. Boston, MA: Beacon.

Hunt, E. K. (1975) *Property and Prophets: The Evolution of Economic Institutions and Ideologies*. New York: Harper and Row.

Hushållningssällskapet (2022) 'REKO-ringar i Sverige'. Available at: https://hushall ningssallskapet.se/forskning-utveckling/reko/ (accessed 31 May 2023).

IPCC (2018) *Global Warming of 1.5°C. An IPCC Special Report on the Impacts of Global Warming of 1.5°C Above Pre-Industrial Levels and Related Global Greenhouse Gas Emission Pathways, in the Context of Strengthening the Global Response to the Threat of Climate Change, Sustainable Development, and Efforts to Eradicate Poverty*. Geneva: IPCC.

Ives, C. D., Freeth, R., and Fischer, J. (2020) 'Inside-out sustainability: The neglect of inner worlds'. *Ambio*, 49:1, 208–217.

Jackson, T. (2016) *Prosperity Without Growth: Foundations for the Economy of Tomorrow*. London: Routledge.

Jackson, T., and Victor, P. (2011) 'Productivity and work in the "green economy": Some theoretical reflections and empirical tests'. *Environmental Innovation and Societal Transitions*, 1:1, 101–108.

Jackson, T. D., and Victor, P. (2013) *Green Economy at a Community Scale*. Toronto: Metcalf Foundation.

Jakobsson, N., Muttarak, R., and Schoyen, M. (2018) 'Dividing the pie in the eco-social state: Exploring the relationship of public support for environmental and welfare policies'. *Environment and Planning C*, 36:2, 313–339.

Jaworek, M., and Kuzel, M. (2015) 'Transnational corporations in the world economy: Formation, development and present position'. *Copernican Journal of Finance and Accounting*, 4:1, 55–70.

Jessop, B. (2002) *The Future of the Capitalist State*. Cambridge: Polity.

Jessop, B., and Morgan, J. (2022) 'The strategic-relational approach, realism and the state: From regulation theory to neoliberalism via Marx and Poulantzas, an interview with Bob Jessop'. *Journal of Critical Realism*, 21:1, 83–118.

Johanisova, N., and Franková, E. (2017) 'Eco social enterprises'. In C. L. Spash (ed.), *Routledge Handbook of Ecological Economics: Nature and Society*. London: Routledge, 507–516.

Johanisova, N., Crabtree, T., and Franňková, E. (2013) 'Social enterprises and non-market capitals: A path to degrowth?' *Journal of Cleaner Production*, 38, 7–16.

Johanisova, N., Surinach Padialla, R., and Parry, P. (2015) 'Co-operatives'. In G. D'Alisa, F. Demaria and G. Kallis (eds), *Degrowth: A Vocabulary for a New Era*. London: Routledge, 152–155.

Kallis, G. (2018) *Degrowth*. Newcastle-upon-Tyne: Agenda.

Kallis, G., Paulson, S., D'Alisa, G., and Demaria, F. (2020) *The Case for Degrowth*. Hoboken: John Wiley and Sons.

Kaufmann, N., Sanders, C., and Wortmann, J. (2019) 'Building new foundations: The future of education from a degrowth perspective'. *Sustainability Science*, 14, 931–941.

Kazepov, Y. (ed.) (2010) *Rescaling Social Policies: Towards Multilevel Governance in Europe*. Farnham: Ashgate.

Keil, A. K., and Kreinin, H. (2022) 'Slowing the treadmill for a good life for All? German trade union narratives and social-ecological transformation'. *Journal of Industrial Relations*, 64:4, 564–584.

Khan, J., Emilsson, K., Fritz, M., Koch, M., Hildingsson, R., and Johansson, H. (2022) 'Ecological ceiling and social floor: Public support for eco-social policies in Sweden'. *Sustainability Science*, 18, 1519–1532.

Kinderman, D. (2017) 'Challenging varieties of capitalism's account of business interests: Neoliberal think-tanks, discourse as a power resource and employers' quest for liberalization in Germany and Sweden'. *Socio-Economic Review*, 15:3, 587–613.

Klitgaard, K. (2013) 'Heterodox political economy and the degrowth perspective'. *Sustainability*, 5:1, 276–297.

Koch, M. (2011) 'Poulantzas's class analysis'. In A. Gallas, L. Bretthauer, J. Kannankulam and I. Stützle (eds), *Reading Poulantzas*. London: Merlin, 107–121.

Koch, M. (2012) *Capitalism and Climate Change*. New York: Palgrave.

Koch, M. (2015) 'Climate change, capitalism and degrowth trajectories to a global steady-state economy'. *International Critical Thought*, 5:4, 439–452.

Koch, M. (2017) *Roads to Post-Fordism. Labour Markets and Social Structures in Europe*, 2nd ed. London: Routledge.

Koch, M. (2018a) 'The naturalisation of growth: Marx, the regulation approach and Bourdieu'. *Environmental Values*, 27:1, 9–27.

Koch, M. (2018b) 'Sustainable welfare, degrowth and eco-social policies in Europe'. In V. Varnhercke, D. Ghailani and S. Sabato (eds), *Social Policy in the European Union: State of Play*. Brussels: European Trade Union Institute, 35–59.

Koch, M. (2019a) 'Growth and degrowth in Marx's Critique of Political Economy'. In E. Chertkovskaya, A. Paulsson and S. Barca (eds), *Towards a Political Economy of Degrowth*. London: Rowman and Littlefield, 69–82.

Koch, M. (2019b) 'Growth strategies and consumption patterns in transition: From Fordism to finance-driven capitalism'. In O. Mont (ed.), *A Research Agenda for Sustainable Consumption Governance*. Cheltenham: Edward Elgar, 35–49.

Koch, M. (2020a) 'Structure, action and change: A Bourdieusian perspective on the preconditions for a degrowth transition'. *Sustainability: Science, Practice and Policy*, 16:1, 4–14.

Koch, M. (2020b) 'The state in the transformation to a sustainable postgrowth economy'. *Environmental Politics*, 29:1, 115–133.

Koch, M. (2022a) 'State-civil society relations in Gramsci, Poulantzas and Bourdieu: Strategic implications for the degrowth movement'. *Ecological Economics*, 193, 107275.

Koch, M. (2022b) 'Social policy without growth: Moving towards sustainable welfare states'. *Social Policy and Society*, 21:3, 447–459.

Koch, M., and Buch-Hansen, H. (2021) 'In search of a political economy of the postgrowth era'. *Globalizations*, 18:7, 1219–1229.

Koch, M., and Fritz, M. (2014) 'Building the eco-social state: Do welfare regimes matter?' *Journal of Social Policy*, 43:4, 679–703.

Koch, M. and Mont, O. (eds) (2016) *Sustainability and the Political Economy of Welfare*. London: Routledge.

Koch, M., Buch-Hansen, H., and Fritz, M. (2017) 'Shifting priorities in degrowth research: An argument for the centrality of human needs'. *Ecological Economics*, 138, 74–81.

Koch, M., Lindellee, J., and Alkan-Olsson, J. (2021) 'Beyond growth imperative and neoliberal doxa: Expanding alternative societal spaces through deliberative citizen forums on needs satisfaction'. *Real-World Economics Review*, 96, 168–183.

Komlosy, A. (2018) *Work: The Last 1,000 Years*. London: Verso.

Kotz, D. M. (2010) 'The final conflict: What can cause a system-threatening crisis of capitalism?' *Science and Society*, 74:3, 362–379.

Kotz, D. M., and McDonough, T. (2010) 'Global neoliberalism and the contemporary social structure of accumulation'. In T. McDonough, M. Reich and D. M. Kotz (eds), *Contemporary Capitalism and its Crises: Social Structure of Accumulation Theory for the 21st Century*. Cambridge: Cambridge University Press, 93–120.

Krippner, G. R. (2005) 'The financialization of the American economy'. *Socio-Economic Review*, 3:2, 173–208.

Kumar, K. (1993) 'Civil society: An inquiry into the usefulness of an historical term'. *British Journal of Sociology*, 44: 3, 375–395.

Lamb, W., and Steinberger, J. (2017) 'Human well-being and climate change mitigation'. *Wiley Interdisciplinary Reviews-Climate Change*, 8:6, 16.

Laruffa, F. (2022) 'Re-thinking work and welfare for the social-ecological transformation'. *Sociologica*, 16:1, 123–151.

Lassila, M. M. (2018) 'Mapping mineral resources in a living land: Sami mining resistance in Ohcejohka, northern Finland'. *Geoforum*, 96, 1–9.

Latouche, S. (2009) *Farewell to Growth*. Cambridge: Polity.

Lawn, P. (2011) 'Is steady-state capitalism viable? A review of the issues and an answer in the affirmative'. *Annals of the New York Academy of Sciences*, 1219:1, 1–25.

Lawson, T. (2015) 'The nature of the firm and peculiarities of the corporation'. *Cambridge Journal of Economics*, 39:1, 1–32.

Lawson, T. (2019) *The Nature of Social Reality: Issues in Social Ontology*. London: Routledge.

Lee, J., Koch, M., and Alkan-Olsson, J. (2023) 'Deliberating a sustainable welfare–work nexus'. *Politische Vierteljahresschrift (German Political Science Quarterly)*. https://doi.org/10.1007/s11615-023-00454-6.

Leonardi, E. (2019) 'Bringing class analysis back in: Assessing the transformation of the value-nature nexus to strengthen the connection between degrowth and environmental justice'. *Ecological Economics*, 156, 83–90.

Leopold, A. (1949) *A Sand County Almanac*. New York: Ballantine.

Lessenich, S. (2019) *Living Well at Others' Expense: The Hidden Costs of Western Prosperity*. Cambridge: Polity.

Liegey, V., and Nelson, A. (2020) *Exploring Degrowth: A Critical Guide*. London: Pluto.

Lindellee, J., Alkan Olsson, J., and Koch, M. (2021) 'Operationalizing sustainable welfare and co-developing eco-social policies by prioritizing human needs'. *Global Social Policy*, 21:2, 328–331.

Lipietz, A. (1992) *Towards a New Economic Order: Postfordism, Ecology and Democracy*. Cambridge: Polity.

Loewen, B. (2022) 'Revitalizing varieties of capitalism for sustainability transitions research: Review, critique and way forward'. *Renewable and Sustainable Energy Reviews*, 162, 112432.

Luxemburg, R. (1951) *The Accumulation of Capital*. New York: Monthly Review Press.

Macy, J., and Johnstone, C. (2022) *Active Hope. How to Face the Mess We're In with Unexpected Resilience and Power*. Novato: New World Library.

Maddison, A. (2001) *The World Economy. A Millennial Perspective*. Paris: OECD.

Maddison, A. (2007) *Contours of the World Economy, 1–2030 AD*. Oxford: Oxford University Press.

Malm, A. (2018) *The Progress of this Storm: Nature and Society in a Warming World*. London: Verso.

Martin, F., de Wilmars Sybille, M., and Kevin, M. (2023) 'Unlocking the potential of income and wealth caps in post-growth transformation: A framework for improving policy design'. *Ecological Economics*, 208, 107788.

Marx, K. (1875) *Critique of the Gotha Programme*. www.marxists.org/archive/marx/works/1875/gotha/ (accessed 31 May 2023).

Marx, K. (1973) *Grundrisse. Foundations of the Critique of Political Economy (Rough Draft)*. Harmondsworth: Penguin.

Marx, K. (1977) *Economic and Philosophic Manuscripts of 1844*. London: Lawrence and Wishart.

Marx, K. (1990) *Capital: A Critique of Political Economy*. Vol. 1. London: Penguin Classics.

Marx, K. (2006) *Capital: A Critique of Political Economy*. Vol. 3. London: Penguin Classics.

Max-Neef, M. (1991) *Human Scale Development: Conception, Application and Further Reflections*. London: Apex.

Max-Neef, M. A. (1992) *From the Outside Looking in: Experiences in 'Barefoot Economics'*. London: Zed.

May, R. (2009) *Man's Search for Himself*. New York: W.W. Norton.

McDonough, T., Reich, M., and Kotz, D. M. (eds) (2010) *Contemporary Capitalism and its Crises*. Cambridge: Cambridge University Press.

Meadows, D. H., Meadows, D. H., Randers, J., and Behrens III, W. W. (1972) *The Limits to Growth: A Report to the Club of Rome*. New York: Universe.

Mete, S., and Xue, J. (2021) 'Integrating environmental sustainability and social justice in housing development: Two contrasting scenarios'. *Progress in Planning*, 151, 100504.

Midgley, M. (2003) *Heart and Mind*. London: Routledge.

Mill, J. S. (1848) *Principles of Political Economy with Some of their Applications*. Whitefish: Kessinger.

Moore, J. M. (2017) 'The Capitalocene, Part I: On the nature and origins of our ecological crisis'. *Journal of Peasant Studies*, 44:3, 594–630.

Moore, M. L, Tjornbo, O., Enfors, E., Knapp, C., Hodbod, J., Baggio, J. A., … and Biggs, D. (2014) 'Studying the complexity of change: Toward an analytical framework for understanding deliberative social-ecological transformations'. *Ecology and Society*, 19:4, 54.

Morgan, J. (2016) 'Paris COP 21: Power that speaks the truth?' *Globalizations*, 13:6, 943–951.

Morgan, J. (2021) 'Critical realism for a time of crisis? Buch-Hansen and Nielsen's twenty-first century CR'. *Journal of Critical Realism*, 20:3, 300–321.

Mote, F. W. (1989) *Intellectual Foundations of China*, 2nd ed. New York: McGraw-Hill.

Næss, A. (1990) *Ecology, Community and Lifestyle: Outline of an Ecosophy*. Cambridge: Cambridge University Press.

Næss, P. (2010) 'The dangerous climate of disciplinary tunnel vision'. In R. Bhaskar, C. Frank, K. G. Høyer, P. Næss and J. Parker (eds), *Interdisciplinarity and Climate Change – Transforming Knowledge and Practice for Our Global Future*. London: Routledge, 68–98.

Næss, A. (2016) *The Ecology of Wisdom*. London: Penguin Classics.

Neilson, D. (2020) 'Bringing in the neoliberal model of development'. *Capital and Class*, 44:1, 85–108.

Neisser, U. (1988) 'Five kinds of self-knowledge'. *Philosophical Psychology*, 1:1, 35–59.

Nesterova, I. (2020a) 'Degrowth business framework: Implications for sustainable development'. *Journal of Cleaner Production*, 262, 121382.

Nesterova, I. (2020b) 'Small business transition towards degrowth'. (PhD thesis, University of Derby.)

Nesterova, I. (2021a) 'Small firms as agents of sustainable change'. *Futures*, 127, 102705.

Nesterova, I. (2021b) 'Small, local, and low-tech firms as agents of sustainable change'. In P. Heikkurinen and T. Ruuska (eds), *Sustainability Beyond Technology: Philosophy, Critique, and Implications for Human Organization*. Oxford: Oxford University Press, 230–253.

Nesterova, I. (2021c) 'Addressing the obscurity of change in values in degrowth business'. *Journal of Cleaner Production*, 315, 128152.

Nesterova, I. (2022a) 'Degrowth perspective for sustainability in built environments'. *Encyclopedia*, 2, 466–472. https://doi.org/10.3390/encyclopedia2010029.

Nesterova, I. (2022b) 'Business of deep transformations: How can geography contribute to the understanding of degrowth business'. *Geography and Sustainability*. https://doi.org/10.1016/j.geosus.2022.03.004.

Nesterova, I. (2022c) 'Being in the world locally: Degrowth business, critical realism, and humanistic geography'. *Frontiers in Sustainability*, 3, 829848.

Nesterova, I. (2023) 'Being of deep transformations: A personal journey inspired by Clive L. Spash'. *Environmental Values* (early view).

Nesterova, I., and Buch-Hansen, H. (2023) 'Degrowth and the circular economy: Reflecting on the depth of business circularity'. *Journal of Cleaner Production*, 414, 137639.

Nesterova, I., and Robra, B. (2022) 'Business in a strongly sustainable society?' In D. D'Amato, A. Toppinen and R. Kozak (eds), *The Role of Business in Global Sustainability Transformations*. London: Routledge.

Nørgård, J. S. (2013) 'Happy degrowth through more amateur economy'. *Journal of Cleaner Production*, 38, 61–70.

Offe, C. (1984) *Contradictions of the Welfare State*. London: Hutchinson.

O'Neill, D. W., Fanning, A. L., Lamb, W., and Steinberger, J. (2018) 'A good life for all within planetary boundaries'. *Nature Sustainability*, 1, 88–95.

Otto, A., and Gugushvili, D. (2020) 'Eco-social divides in Europe: Public attitudes towards welfare and climate change policies'. *Sustainability*, 12:1, 404.

Ougaard, M. (2016) 'The reconfiguration of the transnational power bloc in the crisis'. *European Journal of International Relations*, 22:2, 459–482.

Ougaard, M. (2018) 'The transnational state and the infrastructure push'. *New Political Economy*, 23:1, 128–144.

Overbeek, H. (2013) 'Transnational historical materialism'. In R. Palan (ed.), *Global Political Economy: Contemporary Theories*. London: Routledge, 168–183.

Overbeek, H., and Van der Pijl, K. (1993) 'Restructuring capital and restructuring hegemony: Neoliberalism and the unmaking of the post-war order'. In H. Overbeek (ed.), *Restructuring Hegemony in the Global Political Economy*. London: Routledge, 1–27.

Parker, M. (2018) *Shut Down the Business School: What's Wrong with Management Education*. London: Pluto.

Parker, S. C. (2018) *The Economics of Entrepreneurship*, 2nd ed. Cambridge: Cambridge University Press.

Paulsson, A. (2019) 'The limits of systems: Economics, management, and the problematization of growth during the Golden Age of Capitalism'. In E. Chertkovskaya, A. Paulsson and S. Barca (eds), *Towards a Political Economy of Degrowth*. London: Rowman and Littlefield, 21–38.

Peck, J. (2010) *Constructions of Neoliberal Reason*. Oxford: Oxford University Press.

Perlman, F. (1983) *Against His-Story, Against Leviathan*. Detroit, MI: Black and Red.

Piletic, A. (2019) 'Variegated neoliberalization and institutional hierarchies: Scalar recalibration and the entrenchment of neoliberalism in New York City and Johannesburg'. *Environment and Planning A: Economy and Space*, 51:6, 1306–1325.

Pilisuk, M., and Joy, M. (2015) 'Humanistic psychology and ecology'. In K. J. Schneider, J. Fraser Pierson and J. F. T. Bugental (eds), *The Handbook of Humanistic Psychology: Theory, Research, and Practice*, 2nd ed. London: Sage, 135–147.

Pizzigati, S. (2018) *The Case for a Maximum Wage*. Cambridge: Polity.

Polkinghorne, D. E. (2015) 'The self and humanistic psychology'. In K. J. Schneider, J. Fraser Pierson and J. F .T. Bugental (eds), *The Handbook of Humanistic Psychology: Theory, Research, and Practice*, 2nd ed. London: Sage, 87–104.

Poulantzas, N. (1968) *Political Power and Social Classes*. London: Verso.

Poulantzas, N. (1978) *State, Power and Socialism*. London: NLB.

Puller, A., and Smith, T. (2017) 'A critical and realist approach to ecological economics'. In C. L. Spash (ed.), *Routledge Handbook of Ecological Economics: Nature and Society*. London: Routledge, 17–26.

Purser, R. E. (2019) *McMindfulness: How Mindfulness became the New Capitalist Spirituality*. London: Repeater.

Raworth, K. (2017) *Doughnut Economics: Seven Ways to Think Like a 21st-Century Economist*. London: Random House Business.

Regan, T. (1981) 'The nature and possibility of an environmental ethic'. *Environmental Ethics*, 3:1, 19–34.

Robinson, D. W. (1977) 'The human potential movement'. *The Phi Delta Kappan*, 58:8, 636–638.

Robinson, W. I. (2004) *A Theory of Global Capitalism. Production, Class, and State in a Transnational World*. London: Johns Hopkins University Press.

Robinson, W. I. (2014) *Global Capitalism and the Crisis of Humanity*. Cambridge: Cambridge University Press.

Rockström, J., Steffen, W., Noone, K., Persson, Å., Chapin III, F. S., Lambin, E. F., … and Foley, J. A. (2009) 'A safe operating space for humanity'. *Nature*, 461, 472–475.

Rodman, J. (1983) 'Four forms of ecological consciousness reconsidered'. In D. Scherer and T. Attig (eds), *Ethics and the Environment*. Englewood Cliffs, NJ: Prentice-Hall, 82–92.

Roman-Alcalá, A. (2017) 'Looking to food sovereignty movements for post-growth theory'. *Ephemera*, 17:1, 119–145.

Røpke, I. (2004) 'The early history of modern ecological economics'. *Ecological Economics*, 50:3–4, 293–314.

Røpke, I. (2009) 'Theories of practice: New inspiration for ecological economic studies in consumption'. *Ecological Economics*, 68:10, 2490–2497.

Roszak, T., Gomes, M. E., and Kanner, A. D. (eds) (1995) *Ecopsychology: Restoring the Earth, Healing the Mind*. San Francisco: Sierra Club.

Runciman, D. (2018) *How Democracy Ends*. London: Profile.

Russell, B. (1994) *In Praise of Idleness*. London: Routledge.

Ruuska, T. and Heikkurinen, P. (2021) 'Technology and sustainability: An introduction'. In P. Heikkurinen and T. Ruuska (eds), *Sustainability Beyond Technology: Philosophy, Critique, and Implications for Human Organization*. Oxford: Oxford University Press, 1–26.

Sabato, S., Mandelli, M., and Vanhercke, B. (2021) *The Socio-Ecological Dimension of the EU Recovery: From the European Green Deal to the Recovery and Resilience Facility*. Madrid: EUROsociAL Programme, EUROsociAL Collection No. 24.

Saito, K. (2023) *Marx in the Anthropocene. Towards the Idea of Degrowth Communism*. Cambridge: Cambridge University Press.

Sartre, J-P. (2000) *Nausea*. London: Penguin.

Savini, F. (2023) 'Futures of the social metabolism: Degrowth, circular economy and the value of waste'. *Futures*, 150, 103180.

Sayer, A. (2011) *Why Things Matter to People: Social Science, Values and Ethical Life*. Cambridge: Cambridge University Press.

Schmelzer, M. (2016) *The Hegemony of Growth: The OECD and the Making of the Economic Growth Paradigm*. Cambridge: Cambridge University Press.

Schmelzer, M., Vetter, A., and Vansintjan, A. (2022) *The Future is Degrowth – A Guide to a World Beyond Capitalism*. London: Verso.

Schmid, B. (2018) 'Structured diversity: A practice theory approach to post-growth organisations'. *Management Revue*, 29:3, 281–310.

Schmid, B. (2020) *Making Transformative Geographies: Lessons from Stuttgart's Community Economy*. Bielefeld: Transcript.

Schmid, B. (2022) 'What about the city? Towards an urban post-growth research agenda'. *Sustainability*, 14:19, 11926.

Schneider, F., Kallis, G., and Martinez-Alier, J. (2010) 'Crisis or opportunity? Economic degrowth for social equity and ecological sustainability'. *Journal of Cleaner Production*, 18:6, 511–518.

Schneider, K. J., Fraser Pierson, J., and Bugental, J. F. T. (eds) (2015) *The Handbook of Humanistic Psychology: Theory, Research, and Practice*, 2nd ed. London: Sage.

Schoppek, D. E. (2020) 'How far is degrowth a really revolutionary counter movement to neoliberalism?' *Environmental Values*, 29:2, 131–151.

Schor, J. (2015) 'Work sharing'. In G. D'Alisa, F. Demaria and G. Kallis (eds), *Degrowth. A Vocabulary for a New Era*. London: Routledge, 195–197.

Schumacher, E. F. (1993) *Small is Beautiful: A Study of Economics as if People Mattered*. London: Vintage Random House.

Schumpeter, J. (1947) *Capitalism, Socialism, and Democracy*. New York and London: Harper and Brothers.

Sessions, G. (ed.) (1995) *Deep Ecology for the 21st Century: Readings on the Philosophy and Practice of the New Environmentalism*. London: Shambhala.

Sewell Jr., W. H. (2008) 'The temporalities of capitalism'. *Socio-Economic Review*, 6:3, 517–537.

Shonfield, A. (1965) *Modern Capitalism*. Oxford: Oxford University Press.

Shove, E., Pantzar, M., and Watson, M. (2012) *The Dynamics of Social Practice. Everyday Life and How it Changes*. London: Sage.

Skrbina, D., and Kordie, R. (2021) 'Creative reconstruction of the technological society: A path to sustainability'. In P. Heikkurinen and T. Ruuska (eds), *Sustainability Beyond Technology: Philosophy, Critique, and Implications for Human Organization*. Oxford: Oxford University Press, 254–276.

Skyrman, V. (2022) 'Industrial restructuring, spatio-temporal fixes and the financialization of the North European forest industry'. *Competition and Change*, 27:5, 748–769.

Smith, A. (1976) *An Inquiry into the Nature and Causes of the Wealth of Nations*. Oxford: Oxford University Press.

Söderbaum, P. (2008) *Understanding Sustainability Economics: Towards Pluralism in Economics*. London: Earthscan.

Softas-Nall, S., and Woody, W. D. (2017) 'The loss of human connection to nature: Revitalizing selfhood and meaning in life through the ideas of Rollo May'. *Ecopsychology*, 9:4, 241–252.

Soper, K. (2020) *Post-Growth Living: For an Alternative Hedonism*. London: Verso.

Spangenberg, J. H. (2016) 'The world we see shapes the world we create: How the underlying worldviews lead to different recommendations from environmental and ecological economics – The green economy example'. *Journal of Sustainable Development*, 19:2, 127–146.

Spash, C. L. (1993) 'Economics, ethics, and long-term environmental damages'. *Environmental Ethics*, 15:2, 117–132.

Spash, C. L. (2012) 'New foundations for ecological economics'. *Ecological Economics*, 77, 36–47.

Spash, C. L. (ed.) (2017) *Routledge Handbook of Ecological Economics: Nature and Society*. London: Routledge.

Spash, C. L. (2020) 'A tale of three paradigms: Realising the revolutionary potential of ecological economics'. *Ecological Economics*, 169, 106518.

Spencer, D. A. (2022) *Making Light Work: An End to Toil in the Twenty-First Century*. Cambridge: Polity.

Stahl, R. M. (2019) 'Ruling the interregnum: Politics and ideology in nonhegemonic times'. *Politics and Society*, 47:3, 333–360.

Staricco, J. I. (2017) 'Transforming or reproducing conventional socioeconomic relations? Introducing a regulationist framework for the assessment of fairtrade'. *World Development*, 93, 206–218.

Steffen, W., Richardson, K., Rockström, J., Cornell, S. E., Fetzer, I., Bennett, E. M., ... and Sörlin, S. (2015) 'Planetary boundaries: Guiding human development on a changing planet'. *Science*, 347, 6223.

Stirner, M. (2005) *The Ego and His Own: The Case of the Individual Against Authority*. Mineola, NY: Dover.

Stockhammer, E. (2011) 'Neoliberalism, income distribution and the causes of the crisis'. In P. Arestis, R. Sobreira and J. L. Oreiro (eds), *The Financial Crisis*. New York: Palgrave, 234–258.

Streeck, W. (2000) 'Competitive solidarity: Rethinking the European social model'. *Kontingenz und Krise: Institutionenpolitik in kapitalistischen und postsozialistischen Gesellschaften*. Frankfurt aM: Campus, 245–262.

Streeck, W. (2016) *How will Capitalism End? Essays on a Failing System*. London: Verso.

Swift, R. (2014) *S.O.S.: Alternatives to Capitalism*. Oxford: New Internationalist.

Thoreau, H. D. (2016) *Walden*. New York: Pan Macmillan.

Tilsted, J. P., Mah, A., Nielsen, T. D., Finkill, G., and Bauer, F. (2022) 'Petrochemical transition narratives: Selling fossil fuel solutions in a decarbonizing world'. *Energy Research and Social* Science, 94, 102880.

Trainer, T. (2012) 'De-growth: Do you realise what it means?' *Futures*, 44, 590–599.

Trainer, T. (2014) 'The degrowth movement from the perspective of the Simpler Way'. *Capitalism Nature Socialism*, 26:2, 58–75.

Trainer, T. (2020) 'De-growth: Some suggestions from the Simpler Way perspective'. *Ecological Economics*, 167, 106436.

Trainer, T. (2022) 'A technical critique of the Green New Deal'. *Ecological Economics*, 195, 107378.

Tuan, Y.-F. (1974) *Topophilia: A Study of Environmental Perception, Attitudes, and Values*. New York: Columbia University Press.

Tuan, Y-F (1979) 'Space and place: Humanistic perspective'. In S. Gale and G. Olsson (eds), *Philosophy in Geography*. Dordrecht: D. Reidel, 387–427.

Tuan, Y-F. (1998) *Escapism*. Baltimore, MD: Johns Hopkins University Press.

Tuan, Y.-F. (2001) *Space and Place: The Perspective of Experience*. Minneapolis: University of Minnesota Press.

Tuan, Y-F. (2008) *Human Goodness*. London: University of Wisconsin Press.

Tuan, Y-F. (2013) *Romantic Geography: In Search of the Sublime Landscape*. Madison: University of Wisconsin Press.

UN (2015) *Transforming Our World: The 2030 Agenda for Sustainable Development*. Resolution adopted by the General Assembly on 25 September 2015, United Nations.

van Apeldoorn, B. (2002) *Transnational Capitalism and the Struggle over European Integration*. London: Routledge.

van Apeldoorn, B., and Overbeek, H. (2012) 'The life course of the neoliberal project and the global crisis'. In B. van Apeldoorn and H. Overbeek (eds), *Neoliberalism in Crisis*. New York: Palgrave, 1–20.

van Parijs, P. and Vanderborght, Y. (2017) *Basic Income: A Radical Proposal for a Free Society and a Sane Economy*. Cambridge, MA: Harvard University Press.

van der Pijl, K. (1998) *Transnational Classes and International Relations*. London: Routledge.

van Deurzen, E., and Adams, M. (2016) *Skills in Existential Counselling and Psychotherapy*, 2nd ed. London: Sage.

Vandeventer, J. S., and Lloveras, J. (2021) 'Organizing degrowth: The ontological politics of enacting degrowth in OMS'. *Organization*, 28:3, 358–379.

Wallerstein, I. (2000) 'A Left Politics for the 21st Century? or, Theory and Praxis Once Again'. *New Political Science*, 22:2, 143–159.

Wallerstein, M., and Western, B. (2000) 'Unions in decline? What has changed and why'. *Annual Review of Political Science*, 3:1, 355–377.

Weber, M. (1958) *The Protestant Ethic and the Spirit of Capitalism*. London: Routledge.

Weber, M. (1991) 'Politics as a vocation'. In H. Gerth and C. Wright Mills (eds), *From Max Weber: Essays in Sociology*. London: Routledge, 77–128.

Wigger, A. (2019) 'The new EU industrial policy: Authoritarian neoliberal structural adjustment and the case for alternatives'. *Globalizations*, 16:3, 353–369.

Wigger, A., and Buch-Hansen, H. (2013) 'Competition, the global crisis, and alternatives to neoliberal capitalism: A critical engagement with anarchism'. *New Political Science*, 35:4, 604–626.

Wigger, A., and Buch-Hansen, H. (2014) 'Explaining (missing) regulatory paradigm shifts. EU competition regulation in times of economic crisis'. *New Political Economy*, 19:1, 113–137.

Wilkin, P., and Boudeau, C. (2015) 'Public participation and public services in British liberal democracy: Colin Ward's anarchist critique'. *Environment and Planning C*, 33, 1325–1343.

Woiwode, C., Schäpke, N., Bina, O., Veciana, S., Kunze, I., Parodi, O., Schweizer-Ries, P., and Wamsler, C. (2021) 'Inner transformation to sustainability as a deep leverage point: Fostering new avenues for change through dialogue and reflection'. *Sustainability Science*, 16:3, 841–858.

Wright, E. O. (1994) *Interrogating Inequality: Essays on Class Analysis, Socialism and Marxism*. London: Verso.

Xue, J. (2021) 'Urban planning and degrowth: A missing dialogue'. *Local Environment*, 27:4, 404–422.

Zimmermann, K., and Graziano, P. (2020) 'Mapping different worlds of eco-welfare states'. *Sustainability*, 12:5, 1819.

Index

EU authorised representative for GPSR:
Easy Access System Europe, Mustamäe tee 50,
10621 Tallinn, Estonia
gpsr.requests@easproject.com

www.ingramcontent.com/pod-product-compliance
Lightning Source LLC
Chambersburg PA
CBHW052010270326
41929CB00015B/2856